chang

LIVE

better &

LEAD

differently

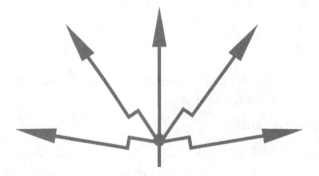

How to Understand Change,
Transforming the Cultures Around Us.

RobRoy Walters

Clovercroft Publishing

change to LIVE better & LEAD differently: How to Understand Change, Transforming the Cultures Around Us.

Published by Clovercroft Publishing, Franklin, Tennessee

Edited by David Brown

Cover Design by Brooke Hawkins

Interior Design by Adept Content Solutions

Printed in the United States of America

978-1-950892-15-0

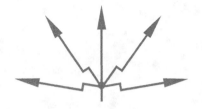

CONTENTS

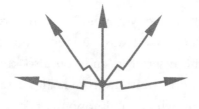

Life Lesson I
CHANGE FROM THE PERSPECTIVE OF A THIRTY-YEAR-OLD LEADER

Closed Doors, Open Opportunities

I was standing in the hallway outside of Regional Bank's (RB) boardroom waiting for the large, wooden double doors to open. There was a meeting already in progress inside the boardroom. It was running a little late and a handful of us were just milling around in the hall, waiting for the room to become available. Most of RB's executive leadership team were in the boardroom participating in the investment committee meeting, which on this day was running over.

I was thirty or thirty-one years old at the time, depending on which month in 1989 this meeting actually took place. In either case, I had only been with RB for a couple months. Hired in as their accounting manager, this was my first meeting with the assembled senior team. Prior to my joining RB, I had spent two years as a staff accountant in Global Resources Corporation's (GRC) Eastern Division Headquarters for the eastern part of the United States. At the time, GRC was one of America's 250 largest corporations. The Eastern Division of GRC focused on the exploration and production of oil and natural gas in several states. For those of you who know me from Books One and Two, you already know that I was a leader in other industries prior to my entry into financial services, and you also know I will go on to lead several different organizations from health care to heavy construction. For those of you who don't know me, take a minute and review "Who is Rob?" at the end of this book. By the way, just as in the prior two books, my use of RB, GRC, and any other companies or people referenced in this book are not being referred to by their real names. The events are certainly real. However, as was the case in my first two books *LIVE better LEAD differently* and *let's all LIVE better & LEAD differently*, I am choosing to put myself in the public eye, but I am not willing to subject others to the same exposure.

This meeting and the events that followed stand out clearly in my memory because of the life lessons rooted in these experiences. What makes them memorable? The emotion. The intense focus of the moment. The ability to recall with clarity a point in time where I was in the position to make a difference, learn a valuable lesson, or discover a truth. Each of these memorable lessons has helped me to develop the materials I shared with you in Books One and Two, and those I am about to share with you now.

Returning to the RB hallway scene, I had been pacing around for about ten minutes and making small talk with a couple other manager-level RB team members when the doors opened and out filed the investment committee members. No one acknowledged those of us standing in the hall. The committee members were all still engaged in side conversations related to the previous meeting. After the boardroom was vacant, those of us who had been waiting went in, found an open seat, and continued to wait until the absent RB executives returned. Before the meeting started, the chief information officer and the vice president of information technology joined us at the table. In about five minutes, the doors were closed and all of the executive team had gathered. At the table, in addition to myself and those I have already mentioned were RB's president and CEO, as well as RB's COO, CFO,

EVP of HR, EVP of trust and investment, chief lending officers, corporate legal counsel, VP of internal audit, and the VP of marketing. The table was full. If you wanted to get something done, anything done within RB, this was the group you would want to gather.

I reported directly to the CFO. He had given me very specific instructions regarding when to speak, what to say, and to stay silent unless I was asked a direct question. If I were asked a question, I was to look to him to see if he wished to answer the question before I was permitted to respond. The information I was told to prepare for the meeting was also very tightly controlled and narrowly defined. I was not to hand out the information to anyone unless the CFO directed me to. I had no idea what the meeting was about. I just knew what I had been ordered to prepare. And, about that, the information I had with me had been reviewed and heavily edited by the CFO. He made multiple changes to the data, which materially altered the support for the conclusions I had reached after doing the research. He justified his changes by explaining to me that I clearly didn't understand the financial services industry. The CFO had been in banking his entire career, and his words to me when I questioned why he made the changes were: "I am a god when it comes to accounting. You just do what you are told!" I found his comments to be both incredibly insulting and wildly entertaining at the same time. I could even see them as being downright humorous if he hadn't been so serious. He actually believed that garbage. I will never forget that meeting. There were so many opportunities for me to observe human behavior and to learn from the experience.

In my short time with RB, I had learned much about the personalities of the executive team, especially the CFO. He had a very aggressive personality. It was "his way or the highway." Most of the executive team were cut from a similar cloth: very intelligent, high energy, in their forties and fifties, and in banking for their entire professional careers. Working in banking for your entire career is perfectly honorable, but in this case, their entire careers had been spent at only one bank, RB. They had already accumulated fifteen to twenty years of tenure within the organization and had climbed their way to the top within their respective divisions. Of those executives I had had a chance to directly observe, the CEO and the EVP of trust and investment were by far the most skilled leaders.

My background up to this point was very different from those seated at the table. Beginning at the age of nineteen, I had spent four years in leadership within one of the nation's fastest growing big-box, discount retailers; then three years selling copiers and office equipment on straight commission; followed by two years finishing my college degree with a major in accounting and finance; and another two years working as a staff accountant within GRC. To say I perceived the world of business differently from the rest of the group would be an understatement. But, I was there to learn the financial services industry, and I *very much* needed this job, so I sat quietly and observed the proceedings with great interest.

I will save the specific topic of the meeting until the latter part of the story, simply for the effect of making my point. Once everyone was seated, the CEO opened the meeting by framing the strategic issue facing us on that day. RB had been approached by a much larger regional bank. This particular bank was one with which we already had multiple banking relations, so their contacting us regarding a joint venture opportunity was not unusual. They had proposed that our two companies work together and construct a different type of information technology (IT) platform in order to better serve our deposit customer base. The IT platform being proposed was one that the bigger bank had successfully put into service within several regional population centers. RB controlled over 50 percent of the deposit market share in its service area, so we were the logical choice to approach with this offer. (For those of you who are not familiar with the banking industry, a 25 percent market share for deposit volume in an area is very significant. RB's control over more than 50 percent of the deposit volume in our markets was huge. In our rural region of south central Ohio, RB was truly the eight hundred–pound gorilla in banking.)

After the CEO framed the business proposal, the CIO weighed in offering his perspective. The CIO was completely against the idea and had a list of reasons as to why this idea would never work and would be a clear and present threat to the integrity of our IT systems. Sharing access to our proprietary programming would surely open a Pandora's box of pending disasters. He was certain that no one seated at the table could support such an unnecessary risk. Once he was finished demolishing the proposal, the other executives lined up in lockstep against the idea. The VP of IT spoke to the numerous difficulties and expenses related to upgrading our IBM mainframe computing platform to accommodate this new service, not to mention the additional programmers that would need to be hired just to keep up with the demands placed on the system by the proposed change.

Internal audit supported the concept of uncontrollable risk. The EVP of HR spoke to how tight we were in space in the IT area and how any increase in the number of programmers would require a remodeling of the entire IT area. Legal was skeptical of the contractual language, but thought they could work through the issues, given time. The VP of marketing saw no need for the addition of this new service to our current deposit-product offerings, especially when you considered the extra cost to RB and in light of all the risks being described. Then, it was time for the CFO to weigh in on the impact from all of the capital expenditures and operating expenses. Down the list of topics I had researched (and he had re-written) the CFO went. Each line item was becoming increasingly more dire and more prohibitive than the last, until finally, he looked in my direction. It was at this point the CFO introduced me to the group as the new accounting manager. He let them know that I did not have a banking background, but he thought that I could learn the "extremely complex business of banking" over time. He then said that I prepared the work he had just quoted, which was only true in the strictest sense. I did not appreciate being tagged as the person responsible for the information the CFO had just delivered to the group, but I sat quietly, letting the comment pass. Patience is a virtue, and I had learned long ago that in leadership, as in life, timing is everything. Learn to wait for the right time.

> *Patience is a virtue; in leadership, as in life, timing is everything.*

Over the next twenty minutes, every other executive at the table, excluding the CEO and the EVP of trust and investment, added their reasons why this was a bad idea for RB and why it would never work. The consensus of those executives weighing in on the proposal was clear. The product would never catch on with our customer base and the costs/risks of entering into this new IT platform were just way too high for RB to even consider it. After all, we already had a 50 percent market share in our region, and this invitation was simply a way for the bigger regional bank to steal our customer base. The CEO then summarized the meeting by saying: *"So, it is pretty clear. It is the **consensus** of the group that we need to reject the offer. Is there anyone in the room that thinks setting up the first Automated Teller Machine (ATM) network within our market is a good idea?"*

Yes, that's right. This discussion was centered on the introduction of the first ATM network into the mostly rural markets we served. At the time this was being discussed by RB, it was a proven technology and had existed in the larger population centers for a few years. As I had researched the technology in preparation for the meeting, I had read about the initial start-up problems and costs, but the level of customer acceptance was exceptional. The problem for those seated at the table was it was simply different, and it represented change from what RB had done in the past. RB was the dominant force in our little corner of the state. "If it ain't broke, don't fix it." This

> *"If it ain't broke, don't fix it." A strategic plan of hundreds of companies, most of which are no longer in business.*

strategic plan has been the mantra of hundreds of companies, most of which are no longer in business.

During my tenure with GRC, the regional VP had, for whatever reason, taken a personal interest in my career. Several times over the prior couple of years, he had called me into his office and discussed the strategic direction of the eastern region as well as global GRC initiatives. This gentleman had been with GRC for several years more than I had been alive and was one of the corporation's most respected executives. One of the projects he asked me to work on was the global integration of GRC's management information system. This project was massive in scope and budget. It impacted almost every aspect of GRC's global operations from inventory tracking, to reserve projections, and to financial measurement and reporting. I had the pleasure of going to our world headquarters in Houston, Texas on multiple occasions and working with some of the company's best and brightest in the areas of IT and finance. Around the table in Houston, I had routinely heard from some of IBM's top systems design people and programmers. When financial options were discussed, it was done by one or more senior level partners from a big eight accounting and consulting firm. GRC's team members were also top-notch. They were highly recruited from all around the country and the world. Granted, around the GRC table, the numbers being thrown around had four or five more zeroes behind them than the RB numbers. It wasn't the difference in cost that stood out to me when I mentally compared the two meetings, but it was the difference in the leadership's attitude toward change.

The GRC project had dwarfed the RB proposal in every way imaginable: cost, complexity, and scope. Besides the difference in attitude toward change, what was particularly striking to me were the conclusions reached by RB's CIO regarding the computing platform required to support the proposed ATM network. Not six months earlier, I had witnessed the IBM engineers and technicians upgrade GRC's in-house IT system from the same basic platform RB was currently using to the new platform being requested to support the ATM network. The global upgrade was done without any major problems. I knew IBM was promoting these types of system upgrades across the country in all business environments. For RB's CIO to focus on system upgrade challenges, quoting IBM as his source for several of the concerns he listed, was surprising to me. I was also puzzled by his constant theme of ongoing security concerns. During the GRC project, security was also a constant topic. All of the voices around the table, internal and external, were focused on system integrity, and all of GRC's concerns had been addressed. The conclusions reached by RB's CIO were curious to me, as were the conclusions of the other executives that had spoken on the topic during the meeting. I had no way to know if they were wrong or GRC was right, or vice versa. I just knew what I had learned through my previous job experience, and I knew what I had read about the new ATM technology in my preparation for this meeting. None of what was going on around the RB table made any sense to me, and I could tell that the CEO was less than pleased regarding the conclusions being reached by his most senior leadership team.

Going back to the CEO's question to the assembled group: *"Is there anyone in the room that thinks setting up the first Automated Teller Machine (ATM) network within our market is a good idea?"* As soon as I heard the question, my hand shot up. It was a reflex action. When I looked around the table, mine was the only supportive opinion being offered.

During most of my previous years of experience, senior leadership actually meant that question when they asked it. My thoughts, as well as anyone else's thoughts regarding the topic at hand, were always welcomed and encouraged. However, at this table, the only person interested in what I had to say was the CEO. Oh, my goodness, if looks could kill, I would have died many deaths in that moment. The CFO, in particular, was obviously not happy with my willingness to join the conversation. Hey, the man seated at the head of the table had just asked us a direct question, and I had a direct answer.

The CEO immediately acknowledged me. Before I began speaking, he welcomed me to the organization. He hoped that I would choose to make banking my career and that I would spend it with RB. Then he asked: *"What is on your mind?"* With that invitation, I gave a brief summary of my relevant experience with GRC and the global integration project I had been a part of. I was careful not to challenge anyone's conclusions directly, out of respect for those in the room and out of respect for the awesome power of corporate politics. Even though I was much younger than everyone else in the room, this wasn't my first high-level meeting, by any stretch. I knew from the looks and body language around the table that I was on very thin ice with almost all of the senior leadership team, and I needed to tread lightly. My comments were carefully restricted in order to focus on my familiarity with this type of conversion, the challenges that may face us, and the opportunities that may be presented if we would re-consider implementing this new technology. After all, taking another look at the project will cost very little, and I offered the name and number of the lead engineer at IBM to our CIO if he wished to call him and discuss the issue.

When I stopped speaking, there was about a fifteen-second pause where you could have heard a pin drop on the carpeted floor. Then the room erupted. *"Apples and oranges. Banking is way more complicated than oil and gas production!" "We don't have all the money in the world to spend on this project. No comparison!"* Similar comments were hurled at me from every corner of the room, except one, the head of the table. The CEO had leaned back in his chair and was watching the spectacle unfold. Specifically, he was watching me as the spectacle unfolded. When I saw him looking at me, I made eye contact and gave him a slight grin, just enough to let him know that I knew a whole lot more about this type of meeting and this particular topic than he had been led to believe. The CEO allowed the blood-letting to continue for about ten minutes.

Then, with a calm tone, he brought the meeting to an abrupt close by saying: *"Well clearly, we are not going to solve this issue here today. Let's meet early next week to finalize the decision. Rob, can I see you in my office please?"* And with that, the meeting was over. The CEO was the first to leave the room.

The CFO immediately came over to me and said: *"The minute he is done with you, I want you in my office!"*

The only other person that spoke to me after that meeting was the EVP of trust and investment. He came up to me with a big smile on his face, shook my hand, and said: *"Welcome to RB!"* You could tell this guy had been entertained by the fireworks, but he and I were the only two seated at the table that saw the humor in the situation.

I gathered my papers and made the short walk to the CEO's office. His administrative assistant asked me to take a seat in the reception area until Mr. E (RB's CEO) was ready for me. In about five minutes, he emerged from his office with a big smile on his face, apologized for keeping me waiting, shook my hand, and asked: *"So, how has your day gone so far?"* Okay, now I knew there were three of us in the room that saw the humor in the situation.

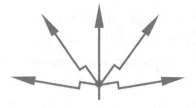

A conversation with the CEO – Part 1

Mr. E closed the door to his office behind us and asked me to be seated at the conference table. *"Well, that was interesting."* These were the first words spoken by Mr. E, setting the tone for that meeting and for my career that followed. My twelve-year career in leadership at RB certainly proved to be "interesting." Mr. E continued: *"Can I get you some coffee? A water?"* "No thank you," I replied. Mr. E poured himself a cup of coffee and joined me at the table.

He continued: *"Tell me about yourself. Why did you decide to join RB?"* With that invitation, I provided him with an expanded, verbal version of my resume. He listened patiently as I told him about life on the farm, my family's ties to the region, my job history, and how my being part of the RB team came to be through my response to a blind ad in the local newspaper.

Mr. E was a tall, slender man. He was soft-spoken and possessed a keen intellect. His professional education was that of an attorney, with a specialization in the laws and structures surrounding estate planning and trust management. Raised on a farm in the northwestern part of Ohio, he had a naturally pleasant demeanor which could quickly put you at ease. He had developed the communication skills needed to project empathy, humility, and respect. Mr. E was passionate about learning and held a deep interest in history. As we sat at the table, he began asking the normal, open-ended questions regarding family, hobbies, and goals.

I shared with him that Jennifer and I were planning to start a family and the career opportunities offered within GRC were very attractive, but would require our relocation to GRC's global head-quarters in Houston Texas. Both Jennifer and I were happy with the quality of life offered here in our part of the country. This quality of life choice is what led me to look for employment opportunities locally. *"I assume that would have paid significantly more than what you are earning here. A difficult choice?"* he asked. I responded: *"Not really. The choice was pretty easy for us. This is our home. For Jennifer and me, it is about what would be best for our family, not about dollars. I learned long ago not to chase money. I am always willing to trade short-term pain for long-term gain."* That answer seemed to peak Mr. E's

> *I am always willing to trade short-term pain for long-term gain.*

curiosity. He began to dig deeper into what was important to me. (Those of you familiar with Book One will recognize this line of questioning as his attempt to gain an understanding of how I answer the all-important question of: "What's in it for me?")

We discussed my core belief structure for leadership. (Leadership Rule #1: Always be professional, which begins with respect for yourself and everyone around you. Leadership Rule #2: Always strive to work smarter, not harder. Leadership Rule #3: Maintain balance in life, have fun!) He uncovered my passion for learning and teaching. We spent time discussing some of the specifics related to the IT project I was part of during my time with GRC. And then, as if he flipped a switch somewhere in his leadership sub-conscience, Mr. E's demeanor changed. During these few short minutes together, he had reached the conclusion that, despite my young age and short time in the financial services industry, I was someone he could work with. Somewhere during our brief conversation, Mr. E concluded that I possessed the strength of character and the level of leadership skill needed to help him grow RB to the next level.

"Now we are going to have a highly confidential conversation," he said as he leaned forward in his chair and dropped the good-old-boy approach to our conversation. I had seen this type of conversational gear-shifting before (Book One) during my dinner conversation with Mr. H when he shifted into what I termed as *full-boss-mode.* Mr. E was making the same conversational shift in order to reinforce an important point. He proceeded to go down the list of RB's senior leadership team. Over his tenure as CEO, Mr. E had recruited and groomed all but a couple of these leaders. Those he had recruited all held advanced degrees, special certifications, or both: CPAs, MBAs, law degrees, CFAs (certified financial planners), etc. The team he had assembled were all intellectually brilliant and all possessed a very high level of energy. These executives formed a solid, homogenous set of Type A personalities. Another characteristic they all shared was an extended tenure with RB. If fact, almost all of the senior leadership team had worked at RB for most, if not all, of their adult lives. They had all worked their way up through the various levels of the organization until they reached the top of their respective divisions.

About forty-five minutes had passed when his administrative assistant knocked on the office door and entered the room. *"Mr. E, you have a board of trustees meeting at the college in thirty minutes,"* she said and then waited for his response. Mr. E responded with: *"Thank you for the reminder, Robin."* She left the room and he turned to me and said: *"I really need to go to this meeting, annual budget stuff. I want to continue our conversation."* I responded with: *"Yes sir. I look forward to it."* As I pushed back from the table and stood up, Mr. E said: *"In about a month, there is a users' group meeting sponsored by our software provider. It is in Orlando, Florida. Usually just Jay (the CIO) and I attend, but I may want you to join us. You interested?"* *"Yes sir, always interested in learning"* was my response. *"Good. I will have Robin get with you regarding flights and schedules. I will be gone the rest of the day. Hope to see you in the morning."* And with that, the meeting was over and he was out the door.

I didn't give any thought to the phrasing of Mr. E's last comment: *"Hope to see you in the morning."* At the age of thirty, with eleven years of leadership experience, I had accumulated enough experience to know that this meeting was, at the least, a rare opportunity for one-on-one time with the CEO. I also had a sense of the potential opportunities being offered with my being invited to attend the users' group conference in Florida.

I thanked Robin and started to walk out of the CEO's suite when she reminded me that the CFO was wanting to see me in his office as soon as my meeting with Mr. E was over. It was a short walk across the hall to my cubicle where I unloaded my meeting materials onto my desk, grabbed a notepad and pencil, and headed back to the CFO's office.

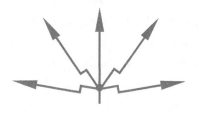

A conversation with the CFO

The CFO's corner office was about fifteen feet square with a single window looking out on to the sea of cubicles which made up RB's accounting and finance areas. There were louvered blinds covering the window that would be closed during confidential conversations. The blinds were wide open as I stepped into his doorway, rapped gently on his door, and said, *"You wanted to see me?"* *"Get in here! Where have you been?! I told you I wanted to see you the minute you were done with Mr. E!"* John shouted as he got up from behind his desk and slammed his office door shut. He pointed to an empty chair in front of his desk and said *"Sit down!"* He continued, *"Do you want to keep your job? Well, do you?"*

John's face was beet red, almost purple, as he paced back and forth behind his cluttered desk. *"I am waiting for an answer!"* I responded, *"Yes sir."* Of course I needed to keep this job! Was he kidding? A few months ago, I had turned down a lucrative offer to relocate to Houston, Texas and continue my career with GRC. My wife and I had just completed designing and building a new home, complete with the obligatory mortgage. We were also planning on starting a family. John knew all of this information from the job interview process. He had one reason and one reason only for beginning the meeting with this particular question. The CFO's weapon of choice was fear, and he was skilled at its application.

Talk about your cultural 180s, wow! Five minutes earlier, I was wrapping up a very positive conversation with the CEO where we ended by planning a trip to a users' conference and now I have my direct supervisor, in a fit of rage, asking me if I want to keep my job. I was wondering where he was going with this performance and I didn't need to wait long to find out.

John reached down to his desk and snatched up a stack of papers. He was holding the papers in his hand and shaking them at me as he spoke: *"You gave me this garbage to work with! I had to fix it before it could be presented in the meeting."* (And with that, he threw the handful of papers at me and they scattered all across the office floor.) *"I saved your butt today and what thanks did I get? I told you not to speak unless I gave you permission! I look across the table and you have your hand up like some first-grader. Pathetic! I have had a half-dozen calls from the other leaders asking me why I can't control you. You really hurt yourself today! If you want to stay, you are going to have to learn to do what you are told. That is the last meeting you will be in for a while!"*

John was obviously an aggressive personality, but even at his worst he couldn't hold a candle to my dad and life on the farm during my last four years at home (more background is available in Book One). Experience had taught me how to quickly evaluate complex situations, like this one, and keep myself calm through the use of simple, easy to remember sayings. The sage advice that was going through my mind during this particular display of silliness was, "When someone insists on acting like a fool, it is always best to get out of their way and let them." There were so many leadership lessons for me to learn during this ridiculous episode, but we weren't finished yet.

> *When someone insists on acting like a fool, it is always best to get out of their way and let them.*

The more I projected calm, the more enraged John became. I sat in the chair across from his desk with my gaze fixed on him. The silence filled the room. After a few seconds, John could take it no more. In what was surely a last-ditch effort to get the desired reaction out of me, he proceeded to take his arm and use it to clear his desk. He sent his stapler flying against the wall and his phone crashing to the floor. Papers were now strewn all across the floor and chairs. I quietly got up from my chair, and proceeded to reach over and pick up his phone. He shouted *"Leave it alone!"* I returned to my chair and sat in silence, keeping eye contact with the CFO. In an intense environment, such as this meeting with John, keeping unbroken eye contact is the non-verbal equivalent of communicating strength of purpose, resolve, and lack of fear. Maintaining eye contact in normal conversations is a non-verbal sign of respect. It is a simple way to show that you are valuing what the other person has to say. But, in this meeting with John, it was intended to communicate my lack of fear. He eventually grew tired of trying to get the desired reaction out of me and began to calm himself down.

His face had turned from glowing purple to a blotchy red. He sat down behind his cleared desk and let out a sigh of disgust. *"I recommended you for this position. I fought to hire you even though you didn't have the qualifications the other execs wanted* (CPA or MBA). *You really let me down today."* With his head in his hands and his face toward the desk, John went on: *"I don't know what I am going to do with this situation. Mr. E called me right after the meeting and he was upset with the way you handled yourself."* John continued: *"I have to spell it out for you, because you will never figure it out on your own. When Mr. E asks the group for other thoughts or opinions, he really doesn't want to hear any. His sole focus is on the leadership team reaching consensus. There is no 'I' in 'Team,' Rob. This isn't about you. It is about RB and our customers. Mr. E doesn't want to see any disagreement around the table. That is why he is so upset with you."* What could I say in response to that line of bull? John's statement regarding Mr. E's being upset with me was in direct contrast with the forty-five minutes I had just spent with the CEO. At this point, I pretty much knew what the CFO was trying to accomplish. His first choice, the use of fear, didn't work in getting me sufficiently rattled, so he switched to another tried-and-true method of manipulation, guilt. And while he was at it, he decided to throw in a little humiliation and condescension for good measure. All in all, John had skillfully delivered a very potent set of manipulation techniques. The problem wasn't his delivery; the problem was his target (me). I had learned long ago to ignore this type of attack, training for years at the foot of a master in the use of fear, intimidation, and condescension... my dad. Thank heavens I had been given the opportunity to learn how to handle this type of foolishness at an early age. I will always be grateful for the life experiences and education my dad provided during my last four years at home.

John stood up from behind his desk and silently headed to the office door. Knowing that the meeting was about to end, I stood up beside my chair. When he reached the door, he pulled it open, put his hand on my shoulder, and said: *"Banking is tough, Rob. It is not for everybody. I want you to really think about your decision to be here. If you decide to leave, I understand. If you decide to stay, you will need to learn how to get along within the RB culture. Now, get back to work. I need to spend the rest of the day trying to fix the problems you have created. Mr. E and I are meeting later this afternoon to talk about you. I hope I can calm him down."* My response was: *"Thank you."* And with that, the meeting was over.

Theater! The entire meeting with the CFO was contrived theater. How did I know it was all an act? Answer: I knew John had deliberately misrepresented the CEO's attitude toward my actions. Plus, I knew there would be no afternoon meeting to "talk about me" because Mr. E was going to be in his board of trustees meeting for the rest of the day. Why did John find it necessary to go through this ridiculous performance? Answer: Control. His purpose was to gain control over my future thoughts and actions through the application of fear and intimidation.

The CFO was well-practiced in the application of fear, as evidenced by the string of accounting managers that had come and gone from RB over the last several years. I was just the next person to occupy the position. John's staged theatrics were clearly designed to gain control over my future actions. I found it all to be completely unprofessional, somewhat educational, and a total waste of time. And what about that poor phone? I bet it had been replaced more frequently than the ill-fated employees who had occupied the accounting manager's position prior to my tenure. Kind of puts a whole new light on RB's choice to use a "blind ad" to advertise the open position in the local paper, doesn't it? (Blind ads don't list the name of the company, only the job description. Interested parties send their resumes to a P.O. Box and only learn the identity of the company if/when they are called for an interview.) Even if I had known the history of the position, which I didn't, I would have still applied in an effort to meet the immediate needs of my family.

As John opened the door to his office, signaling the end of our meeting, my mind was filled with thoughts of others. First and foremost, my thoughts were of my wife, Jennifer, and the potential impact my losing this job would have on our plans. Next, what about those RB employees for whom I was responsible? Surely they heard the entire performance. What a mess! Oh well, you can't un-ring a bell. Time for me to get to work repairing whatever emotional damage that had been inflicted on others. When I got home later that evening, I would discuss the situation with Jennifer, and we would figure it out, as we always do, together. But, the day was not over. Who knows what else may happen?

At the time, there were only a handful of the accounting and finance department team members that reported to me. Most of them had been there for a few years and had seen this all before. Sound traveled easily through the walls surrounding John's office, and my group of direct reports had heard just about every word. Shoot, I bet folks on the sidewalk outside the building also heard John as they walked by. I returned to my cubicle, glanced at the new stacks of paper that had been placed on my desk, flipped my pencil onto my desk, and walked across the hall to get a cup of coffee. There was a kitchenette just outside the boardroom, the same room where this adventure had started just a couple hours earlier. Robin was kind enough to always have fresh coffee ready for anyone who needed a cup (especially for Mr. E or his guests). I filled the Styrofoam cup about half full and leaned back against the countertop, pausing for a moment to gather my thoughts.

At the top of my revised to-do list was to walk the floor (rounding on my direct reports) in order to put them at ease. When I left the CFO's office, there was an eerie silence that had settled over the sea of cubicles. I noticed a lack of the ever-present clicking of calculator and computer keys. Also, there were no ongoing phone conversations; in fact, there were no audible conversations at all. Each person was hunkered down inside the walls of their workspace in an effort to avoid being the next target to show up on John's radar. As we learned in Book One, the use of fear by a leader is an efficient and effective technique for influencing others. From a position of authority, fear is easy to generate, but impossible to control. The analogy I used in Book One was: "Fear has the same effect as tossing a boulder into the middle of a small pool. The splash zone of fear will engulf everyone physically or virtually present in the room. Outside of the splash zone, the negative ripple effect will travel through the organization at the speed of a tsunami." Fear is usually the primary tool of the unskilled or insecure leader, but one should never make the mistake of underestimating its effectiveness.

> *Fear is the primary tool of the unskilled or insecure leader.*

As I took a sip of my coffee, I could only smile. One needs to be able to look beyond the foolishness and see the humor in this type of meeting. I had lived through this type of behavior many times before and from those experiences, I had developed the ability to perceive these attacks as opportunities to better understand human behavior. I was able to emotionally flip the aggressive behavior I was witnessing 180 degrees and view it as a shining reminder of what NOT to do as a person or a leader. However, the CFO's threats were real . Because they were genuine, I needed to quickly figure a way to counteract the negative consequences, which brings me back to the impact on those in the immediate "splash zone."

My first priority was to calm everyone down by letting them see that I was fine. They needed to see that I had no worries and that it was business as usual. After spending a couple minutes collecting my thoughts, I started out of the kitchen to make my rounds when Robin caught my attention. *"There you are,"* she said. *"I left word with Beverly that I needed to see you when you had a minute. You were back with John when I came over."* (FYI, that comment from Robin was specifically designed to let me know that she was aware of what had just transpired.) She continued: *"Do you prefer to fly out of the regional airport or out of Columbus? I can get you a direct flight out of Columbus."* I replied: *"Always prefer a direct flight. Columbus is fine. Thank you for putting all this together, Robin."* Then I asked: *"Will Mr. E be flying out of Columbus?"* Robin responded: *"No. He is flying private out of the regional airport. Mr. E has a seat on their user development board and they always send Mr. K's plane to pick him up. By the way, what is your schedule like in the morning? Mr. E wants to continue your conversation from earlier today when you get in."* I answered with: *"I should be here at my regular time, around 7:30. Whenever he wants to meet is fine with me."* Robin said: *"Put him down on your calendar for 7:30 in the morning. I'll let you know if anything changes."* And with that, she headed back to the CEO's office suite and I headed over to start calming folks down.

I have always suspected that this conversation was strategic, delivered at the direction of the CEO. The next morning, it would become clear to me that Robin and Mr. E had spoken that afternoon. Based on that knowledge, there is no doubt in my mind that Robin delivered to Mr. E a summary of John's tirade. It was the CEO's quick reaction, scheduling a meeting early the next morning, which gave me a sense of comfort. Why did it have a calming impact on me? The message being sent was designed to get my mind off recent events and get me focused on the future. My immediate future held a second meeting with the CEO. Also, Robin scheduling my flight to the user conference provided assurance that Mr. E was looking beyond today. In the years that followed, I have successfully employed this same technique numerous times, helping others to maintain a positive attitude by giving them a reason to look forward, beyond the difficulties of today. Before we get to the opportunities behind the next closed door, allow me a moment to add some needed context regarding the two paragraphs above. First, let's spend a moment discussing Robin.

Robin was the consummate professional, the very definition of an effective executive administrative assistant (admin) and she also served as secretary to the board. She had been with Mr. E for many years and was his trusted right hand. She was highly intelligent, well organized, confidential, and completely loyal to Mr. E and the RB organization. She was blessed with exceptional communication skills and was excellent at quickly evaluating an individual's character. Admins like Robin are exceptional people. They are the foundation on which many successful executives depend. Robin was a critical member of the leadership team.

The other key character I introduced above was "Mr. K." Mr. K (or Keith) was the founder, and held the controlling interest in a large IT company. His company, K Corp, provided the software that RB and many banks across the country used to operate their lending, deposit, and transaction capture functions. At this point in time, Mr. K's company was a massive organization. His company was a leading provider of software to many regional banks in the United States and across several countries around the world. The company was headquartered outside of Orlando FL. A talented entrepreneur, dynamic leader, brilliant visionary, and tireless worker, he had built what was, at the time, the dominate force in the banking software industry. Mr. K was only known to me by reputation. That would change in the not too distant future. But, for now, the task at hand was to offer calm to those who had been caught in the splash zone created by the boulder of fear John had thrown into the RB accounting and finance departments.

As I made my way from cubicle to cubicle, I encountered a variety of reactions. As you would expect, each person responded in their own unique way. One of the ladies was in tears, upset that one person would treat another person in that manner. Another lady calmly looked at me and asked if I was coming back tomorrow. They were already beginning to speculate as to who would be the next accounting manager.

Those were the two extremes. Everyone else displayed some level of apprehension at first, then got right back to work once they saw I was not upset. In short, forty-five minutes later, the entire episode was put into context and folks returned to the normal working environment. If you think about it, the environment I had just witnessed being accepted as "normal" was very sad. Who was to blame for the existence of this environment? Answer: I was responsible. Sure, the CFO certainly played a major role in creation of the culture, as did the CEO through his willingness to tolerate this type of leadership behavior. The other members of the senior leadership team each had a hand in allowing John's behavior to continue. But I was the person responsible for changing the workaday reality for these five individuals. I didn't create the situation, but I owned it.

I can already hear the reactions to this part of the story and my taking ownership of the issue. The behavior of the CFO was clearly unacceptable by today's standards. Actually, his behavior was unacceptable by any leadership standard. His actions stood in direct conflict with Leadership Rule #1: "Always be professional, which begins with respect for yourself and everyone around you." But even if you ignore Rule #1, in today's litigious society, the risk factors created through this type of behavior would force RB's senior leadership to take action to restrain or remove John in order to avoid potential legal action.

Please understand, my actions were the catalyst behind these events. I was specifically told by the CFO not to speak unless asked a direct question and, even if I was asked a direct question, I was to look to him for permission to speak before addressing the group. Clearly, my instinctive reaction to the general inquiry offered by the CEO was in direct violation of those instructions. I was, in point of fact, insubordinate when I volunteered my thoughts to the group. Forget what is reasonable, and set aside the silliness of the reaction. My actions were the root cause for the CFO's display, the cause of the effect. John was reacting to the opportunity I provided. Again, set aside **how** the CFO reacted and focus on the **why** behind

Learning to effectively lead change requires the ability to look beyond the obvious results in order to see the hidden opportunities.

his response. Learning to effectively lead change requires the ability to look beyond the obvious in order to see the hidden opportunities. At this point in the process, I was unable to see beyond the obvious. I didn't know it yet, but I had positioned myself squarely between two powerful cultures which existed within the RB organization. I was defiantly seen as a threat by those (many of the executive team) who wished to maintain the status quo. At the same time, I was perceived as a potential ally by those who were advocating change (the CEO and some key members of the board). Let's take just a moment to label these differing leadership platforms.

When dealing with change, you can choose from three basic types of leadership platforms. We will briefly define each. First, there is the platform for **leading change**. When leading change, the leader is required to be the keeper of the vision. When you lead the process of change, you are responsible for communicating and keeping the focus squarely on the purpose of the change. As a leader of change, one can choose to either facilitate the process or to be the catalyst causing the change. In either case, facilitator or catalyst, you will be the keeper of the vision, the "why."

Next, one can **manage change**. Managing change requires the leader to become an active participant in the actual process of change. Managing change is all about the structure of the change. Here is where you typically find the subject matter experts, those that know the details surrounding the processes and the systems being impacted by the change. These are the "doers." If you are managing change, you are striving to accomplish a defined set of tasks over a specified time period.

And finally, there is **change management**. Change management is the lesser known of the three and the most challenging. Change management requires a leader to possess a combination of skills. Successful change management requires the leader to possess the communication skills of the change leader and the detailed knowledge of the subject matter expert. Change management can call for facilitation skills one minute and technical skills the next. Of the three, change management contains the highest risk and the most potential reward, but not necessarily financial rewards. For now, think of a change manager as the person that forms the communication bridge between the keepers of the vision and those in charge of maintaining structure.

To master change management, a leader must develop the skills necessary to anticipate the *cause and effect* of actions taken during the process of change. At the age of thirty, I had not yet developed the necessary skills to anticipate the full range of effects from my own actions. Shoot, at this early point in my Cycle of Human Development (Books One and Two), I was simply attempting to answer Mr. E's question. It was nothing more complicated than direct Q & A with the CEO.

In addition to the CFO's (a senior member of the group managing change) attention, my actions had an impact on the CEO (the keeper of the vision for leading change). Mr. E's curiosity was engaged when I responded to his question, but his curiosity was piqued by my lack of reaction to the hail of attacks which followed my comments. During our first meeting, he wanted to see if I possessed a set of leadership skills which differed from his current executive team. Mr. E was about to test his first impressions of me through this second meeting. The next morning was going to be very interesting.

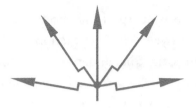

A conversation with the CEO – Part 2

I was at my desk by 7:15 that next morning. Robin had already made the day's first pot of coffee and I was busy working at my desk when I heard a pleasant voice say: *"Good morning."* I looked up and Mr. E was standing at the edge of my workspace. *"Do you have a minute?"* he asked. *"Sure,"* I said and started to grab a notepad and paper. When he saw what I was doing, Mr. E said: *"You won't need those. Just bring your coffee and let's sit down and talk for a few minutes."*

As we walked through the waiting area, I said good morning to Robin and thanked her for making the morning's coffee. Into the CEO's office I stepped for the second time in as many days. The door closed behind me. He headed for the conference table and I joined him. As soon as I was seated, Mr. E said: *"I understand that when you left my office yesterday, you went straight into a meeting with John. Tell me how that went."* Based on yesterday's conversation with Robin, I had anticipated being asked this question. From previous experience gained through personal failure in answering this question, I knew how best to respond. On its surface, the question is constructed as an open-ended invitation to vent. It appears as an invitation to share what were, most likely, unpleasant experiences, when in fact, the question is usually used by skilled leaders as a method for assessing another individual's strength of purpose and leadership maturity.

Here is how this type of question works. If I had taken the opportunity to lay into John, recounting his aggressive and intimidating actions, I would have been speaking the truth and well within my rights as an RB employee. Mr. E's reaction to this type of response would be one of empathy and understanding, followed by a sincere apology and a promise to discuss the incident with John. The CEO would have assured me that John's behavior did not reflect the RB culture and then he would add in something like: "He must have been having a bad day. Again, I apologize for what you have been through and, if it ever happens again, I want you to go straight to HR and discuss it with the employee advocate. I am glad we had this time to talk and thank you for sharing your thoughts. I know it was not easy and I appreciate your honesty." At which point, the meeting would be over and, most likely, my career at RB would be put on hold until I was able to consistently display a higher level of leadership maturity.

The correct way to respond to this question is by following Leadership Rule #1: Always be professional, which begins with respect for yourself and everyone around you. Here is the gist of my answer to Mr. E's question: *"It was interesting. You were right, Mr. E, when during our meeting yesterday, you went through the basic personalities of your executive leadership team. I very much appreciated the heads-up you gave me. Yes, John has a direct style of communication, but I was able to look beyond the theatrics and hear his message. He is very much a command and control leader and I made the mistake of speaking without his giving me permission. My mistake."* Hearing my answer, Mr. E responded: *"You keep on speaking up! I am counting on you to see things differently from the others and to ask better questions. If you make a mistake, you make a mistake. Truth is, if you're not making mistakes, you're not doing anything. I didn't mean to interrupt. Keep going. What else?"* *"I am worried about John's poor phone,"* I said with a smile on my face. *"It took a pretty good shot yesterday. Hope it works today."* That comment got a chuckle out of Mr. E and he commented: *"That's not his first phone and I don't imagine it will be his last."*

I continued: *"There is one thing John said yesterday that has stuck with me. May I ask you what may be a difficult question?"* *"Sure,"* he responded. *"John told me that you expect consensus from your leadership team and that my offering a view that was contrary to the group upset you. I can tell from our conversation this morning that my comments didn't upset you, but is that your expectation? Do you expect consensus from your executive team?"* At that moment, Mr. E broke eye contact with me and glanced down at his coffee cup. In a moment of deep reflection and in a quiet tone, almost a whisper, he answered: *"That's true."* He stood up from the table and began walking to the coffee service set that was in his office. *"More coffee?"* he asked. *"No thank you. I'm good."*

Mr. E resumed: *"Rob, do you know what consensus means?"* I responded with: *"Yes sir, in a word, agreement."* As he poured himself another cup of coffee, he continued: *"Yes, that is a definition of the word, but do you know what it means?"* Not certain as to where he was headed with his comment, I chose to assume it was a rhetorical question and sat silently, waiting for him to continue. *"Let me give you some RB history. When I was interviewing for this job, I immediately saw potential within the RB organization. RB already had a strong market presence; strength on the board; quality of assets; good facilities; minimal competition from the major banks; and the organization was transitioning out several of its key leadership team. I was able to quickly develop a plan. Most importantly, I was able to put forward a **purpose** for RB and presented my **vision** for the future to the board during the interview process. They must have liked it because they hired me and, over the years, they have supported me every step of the way.*

"We were much smaller at that time. As we grew, I recruited key individuals with the necessary technical skills and the drive to lead a larger organization. Over the first few years, we were able to assemble a pretty good team, the core of the executive team we have today. Each leader developed their own leadership style, a style that matched their individual personality, and they had the freedom to lead their areas in the manner they believed to be most effective. I very rarely interfere in the day-to-day operations of their areas, as long as policy is being followed and the results are acceptable. In these first few years, I focused my energy on sharing the vision for the organization with each leader, team member, customer, and shareholder. As the CEO, my daily focus was on building a consensus around our vision.

"During this period, when we were re-structuring RB, putting in a new foundation for the future, the leadership team had more than a few heated disagreements on policy, procedure, and strategy. These were healthy exchanges that brought out the best from all of us, challenging each of us to do more and, most importantly, ask better questions. We always pushed the topic forward by asking and debating the 'Why' behind each decision. Why go in this direction? Why not go in this other direction? I would serve more as a facilitator in these meetings, than the CEO. My job was to prompt everyone to participate, keep the group from getting off track, and to demand consensus from the group regarding the purpose of the decision. I insisted that, whatever course they chose, it was in agreement with our vision. If what the group had developed was contrary to my personal opinion, I would express my opinion as a member of the team and then support the group's decision as long as the entire team formed consensus around our purpose.

"Unfortunately, somewhere along the way, the group lost sight of the true meaning of consensus and replaced 'agreement regarding purpose of vision' with 'agreement on direction.' The team's priorities have shifted more toward accomplishing tasks and minimizing personal risk. This change was gradual and took place over a few years. Frankly, RB's success has made me lazy. My fault! I lost focus on my role as a teacher. Instead of facilitating meetings, I now chair meetings. We stopped asking ourselves 'Why.' Now we focus on how, who, and when."

By this time, Mr. E had returned to his seat beside me at the conference table. I understood exactly what he was saying. I had witnessed this type change in leadership focus at my previous job with GRC and in my first job with the big-box retail store. In both cases, leadership's focus changed, borne out of sustained success. Somewhere along the way, usually as they enter the rarified air of the VP level and above, executives begin to see the process of change as a threat to their personal security. The risk of being found to be wrong becomes an intolerable result. To avoid being found wrong, the executives within both companies began to insulate themselves by forming a protective armor forged out of policies and procedures. They continued to add layers of bureaucracy, increasing the resistance to change, until they thought themselves to be sufficiently protected.

Staring into his coffee cup, Mr. E continued. *"My fault!"* he reported. Mr. E took ownership of RB's current cultural circumstances for a second time, but this time his tone was different. This time, his tone was one of resolve. He continued: *"I helped to get us to where we are today, but you and I are going to put us back on track. Rob, for the first time in my tenure with RB, I am seeing dark storm clouds gathering on the horizon. There are difficult times ahead for the financial services industry, and smaller banks like us will only survive if we learn to be innovative. What we saw yesterday was a missed opportunity for us to increase our chances of surviving the storm. Leveraging technology is the future of banking. We need to leverage technology and put it in the hands of those RB employees who work on the front lines as well as into the hands of our customers. Our passing on the opportunity to build the first ATM system in this market is a mistake. But, in our current culture, if I tried to force the change onto the executive team after they unanimously rejected it, that would be a bigger mistake. Like you said yesterday, Rob, we need to be willing to accept some short-term pain in order to generate a long-term gain.*

"No, what is clear to me now is that we need to make some changes in our leadership team. Our current IT leadership either needs to embrace the concept of pushing technology out to the point-of-service or we need to find new leadership. Either way, I need to make a decision regarding Jay's future role within RB, and soon.

"Did Robin tell you that I am on the user board for K Corporation? Keith K has shown me what the future of technology in banking looks like. He and his team are in the process of building those innovations into a workstation platform. They are focused on leveraging information, and putting it directly into the hands of the teller, loan officer, customer service rep, and branch manager. Everything they are building is focused on delivering value to the customer. That is the future of banking. That is our future! We can either build an infrastructure that will help us to survive the storm that is coming or we will be one of the institutions that will be swept away.

"Your experience at GRC may be helpful to Keith and his team. Even if what you know is not that helpful to K Corp, your spending time with some of his people will be helpful to RB. I need a fresh set of eyes looking at what

*they are developing. I need to know if **you** think that what they are building will actually deliver value to our customers. Over the next few months, I need you to learn what you can about Keith, his company, and the software products they currently offer. Talk with Jay and get a better understanding of our systems, our strengths, our weaknesses, and most importantly, our potential for delivering value to our customers by leveraging this new platform. Any questions?"*

"Yes sir," I replied. And with a smile on my face, I asked: *"I take it from this conversation that I still have a job, right?"*

Mr. E switched into boss mode and replied: *"I assume your question comes out of your meeting yesterday with John. First, whether you stay or go is your decision. I hope you decide to stay. But, if you do, know that there will be many more meetings with John. Some meetings will be fine and some will be as bad as yesterday or worse. If you choose to stay, I won't protect you, but I can open the doors of opportunity for you. What you choose to do with it is up to you. I will tell you this, you have the integrity, courage, and leadership skills needed to help take us to the next level. As time passes and you learn more about banking, specifically RB, I will be very curious to see what you are capable of, and I will be extremely disappointed if you choose to leave before giving yourself some time to learn. You owe it to yourself to at least explore the opportunities RB presents."* With that, he stood up from his chair, shook my hand, then reached over and grabbed a book off his desk. Handing it to me, he said: *"I just finished reading this. You may find it interesting. Ever hear of Peter Drucker? Also, I have a book around here somewhere that introduces the concepts behind TQM* (Total Quality Management) *and reengineering. When I find it, I will get it to you."*

"Yes sir. Thank you," I replied. I walked out of my second meeting with the CEO with reading material in hand, a new set of assignments, and a much better understanding of the man at the helm of the RB ship. I had never heard of Peter Drucker, nor was I familiar with the concepts of TQM or reengineering. It was 1989. I was thirty years old and a graduate of the school of hard knocks. I held a BS in business administration with a major in accounting/finance. Management theory? Change management? Leveraging technology? These questions were not part of who I was at the time and Mr. E knew that. It was time for me to get to work. Time to grow as a leader!

The next couple of months passed quickly. Yes, I was still employed at RB. I found a way to co-exist with John (the CFO) that seemed to work. He truly saw himself as an "accounting god." All I needed to do to get along with John was to acknowledge his accounting skills from time to time. Anytime you are dealing with an ego-driven personality like John's, there will be good days and days that are not so good. The key is to know which days are which and adjust your expectations accordingly.

I had also learned a great deal about Keith K, K Corp, the financial services industry in general, and RB in particular. I was consuming everything I could find on those topics as well as management theory, change management, and the concept of leveraging new technologies in order to place the power of information directly in the hands of the end user. I was fully engaged and progressing along a very steep learning curve.

However, the most important change of all was on the home front. Jennifer was now expecting our first child. All of this change was swirling around me as the door on the plane closed and the jet was pushed back from the terminal. I was leaving Columbus, Ohio and heading to Orlando, Florida. A few hours later, the door on the plane opened and I stepped onto the walkway. Welcome to Orlando. Welcome to another layer of opportunity!

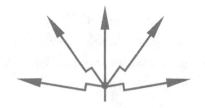

Orlando in October

The Orlando airport is one of the busiest airports in the world. After getting off the plane, I watched and learned from my fellow travelers as they navigated between the terminals. Eventually, I was reunited with my luggage and found myself seated on a private shuttle which was provided by K Corp for the convenience of the user conference attendees. The shuttle pulled up to the front of Orlando World Center Marriott. This was an impressive facility. It was massive in size with first class accommodations. Guests had access to all the amenities necessary for an enjoyable stay. But, playing golf or lounging by one of the pools held no interest to me. I was here to learn. I hopped off the shuttle, checked in, dropped my luggage off in my room, and began to explore my new surroundings. When I had checked in, the front desk provided me with a packet of user conference materials, which included an agenda and a map of the facility. I set out to learn where I was headed in the morning.

Early the next morning, I was standing in line at one of the tables issuing name badges and handing out conference schedules to the attendees. When I eventually reached the table for the "Ws," the young lady looked up and said: *"Good morning. Welcome to K Corp's users conference. Name?"* I replied: *"Good morning. Rob Walters."* *"Would that be RobRoy Walters?"* was her question back to me. *"Yes, that's me. I go by Rob, but RobRoy is my first name."* *"Thank you, Mr. Walters and welcome. I hope you had a good flight."* She then turned and motioned to a gentleman that was standing by one of the many doors that led into the huge room where breakfast was being served. She called out: *"Ish, this is Mr. Walters."* The gentleman immediately joined us at the registration table. *"Good morning, Mr. Walters, I am Ish, a design engineer here at K Corp. Welcome to the user conference. I hope your trip here was uneventful."* I replied: *"Yes, as well as one can hope, and please, I am Rob."* *"Rob, if you follow me, we have your table over here. We will be joined this morning by Roger, K Corp's senior design engineer. I hope you don't mind talking a little business over breakfast this morning."* *"Sounds good to me, Ish. What's for breakfast?"* was my response. Ish chuckled and said: *"Whatever you want, Rob. Whatever you want."*

The table was in the very back of the room, set up in a secluded corner with a "Reserved" sign in the center. It would seat about ten people, but for now, there was just the three of us plus a waiter. None of the other tables appeared to be reserved and certainly no other tables had an assigned waiter. I had read about Roger while studying K Corp's history. He is credited with designing much of what is the current software system used by RB and many banks across the country and around the world. Great! What an opportunity for me to learn, but what is going on here? Why am I sitting down with Ish and Roger at a private table in what was a very public gathering? Oh well, I would learn the answer to "why" soon enough.

We reached the table and Ish made the introductions. Coffee was served and we exchanged the usual pleasantries. I pretty much knew Roger's bio from my pre-trip research. Oxford and MIT educated, this guy was a heavy hitter in tech. We quickly got down to business. The conversation immediately focused on my time at GRC and the global IT project on which I had worked. Roger asked general questions like who we had coordinated with at IBM and what type of design challenges we had run into as we assembled our integrated platform. We spoke for about thirty minutes before breakfast was served. As we ate, we spent a little time exploring my general knowledge of integrated platform technology. However, most of the conversation focused on how I would apply these concepts to a banking application. Specifically, Roger wanted to hear how I thought integrated technologies could be applied to help the RB employees at the front lines of service (the point-of-service or "POS") to deliver greater value to our customers.

As we finished our morning meal, Roger pushed back from the table and said: *"Ish, I am certain you have some questions for Rob. If you will excuse me for a moment. I will be right back."* With that being said, Roger exited the large room through a small door that was built into the partition wall, next to the table. I hadn't even noticed the door until Roger exited through it. During Roger's absence, Ish and I continued to discuss the possible applications for POS technologies. In about ten minutes, the door opened and Roger reappeared, only this time he was not alone.

Trailing Roger through the door was an impeccably dressed gentleman. I recognized him immediately as Keith K, the owner of K Corp. Following Mr. K, there were two other gentlemen, one of whom was a very large man who ducked as he made his way through the door. It was obvious that the second gentleman through the door was personal security. I assumed the third gentleman was a personal assistant. Much like my encounter with Mr. H from Book One, Mr. K greeted me as if he had known me his entire life. *"Good morning, Rob! Are you being treated well? I hope these boys haven't talked too much this morning. Roger tells me that you are the 'real deal.' I was talking with Phil (Mr. E's first name) yesterday while we were out on the lake. He tells me you are someone who will be helpful as we build out the next version of our banking software. Roger tells me that after spending time with you this morning, he sees potential in working with you on the final development of our next release. Ish, do you agree?" "Yes sir, I very much agree,"* Ish replied.

I was seated at the table with my back to the room, so I was not aware that a collection of photographers was beginning to gather. My first clue to the group's presence was when the flashes from their cameras began to illuminate our corner of the room. Mr. K was still speaking, so I did not break eye contact, but I was curious as to what was going on behind me. In mid-sentence, Mr. K interrupted himself, and holding up his right index finger, he said: *"Excuse me for a minute, Rob. Tony, private meeting."* With those words being spoken, the very large man in the finely tailored suit, who had been standing behind Mr. K, stepped around to the front of the table and stood between us and the photographers. Tony spread his arms, and making a herding motion much like my mother used to make when she would coax chickens into the hen house, he gently persuaded the photographers to let this opportunity for pictures pass. Tony resumed his watchful position and Mr. K continued: *"Thanks Tony. Sorry about the interruption, Rob. Those are my marketing people and some local press. They are just doing their job. We have scheduled plenty of time for pictures later. Let's get back to business."*

"We have some of the most talented system designers in the world. I decided long ago that my most important investment is the one I make in our people. K Corp recruits top talent at every position and I am proud of the team we have assembled. But, even with all the talent we have, sometimes we need to seek out a completely different perspective. Someone, like yourself, that can see how to apply the technologies we have created. When we gain new perspectives on how to leverage our product, we can make huge leaps forward in providing value to our customers. Phil has told me about your background, your character, and that you have the courage to ask the right questions.

"Over the next few months, I would like for you to work with us on the application side of our new software design. Phil supports your participating with us and Roger certainly thinks you would bring value to the development team. Most of what we would need from you can be handled remotely, but I will need you to be here in Orlando for next April's technical conference. K Corp will cover all your expenses for the April conference. Bring your family for the week. We will cover the cost of their flight and hotel too. Can I count on you?"

I responded immediately: *"Yes sir! I would welcome the opportunity to learn from your team and I would be more than happy to help in any way I can, but Jennifer and I are expecting a baby in May. So far, knock on wood, she has gotten along just fine. I know you will understand that my priority is with her. I would be concerned about being this far away, and the availability of a return flight, if I needed to get back home in an emergency. Even after I landed in Columbus, I would still be three hours driving time away from the house. Her mom and dad live right down the street, but I am still concerned about being away at that time."*

"Congratulations! Your first?" Mr. K asked. *"Yes sir, our first."* Then Mr. K turned to the other gentleman that came in with him and motioned with his hand, as if he were holding a pen and writing a note in the air. The gentleman responded immediately by handing Mr. K a business card and a pen. He thanked the gentleman, turned the card over, and began writing a note on the back of the card. When he finished, he handed me the card and said: *"Thanks Aaron. Rob, I completely understand and I want you to do whatever makes sense for you and Jennifer. Family first, always. This is Aaron's business card and it contains all his contact information. On the back of the card, I have written the contact information for my personal assistant, April. Between the two of them, we can make almost anything happen. If you are able to join us for the technical conference in April, I will have a car and a jet at your disposal the entire time you are on the ground with us. You say the word and I will have you wheels up in twenty minutes and at your regional airport in two hours. You tell Jennifer that we will have you home in three hours from the time she calls. April will work out the details with Robin."*

As those words exited his mouth, the side door cracked open and a well-dressed lady motioned to Mr. K. He glanced in her direction and acknowledged her request. Mr. K turned back to me, asking: *"Are you coming to the barbeque this evening? Great food and entertainment. That lady right there has worked hard to make certain that it will be a night to remember. Trust me, you don't want to disappoint her."*

"No sir, I can't attend. I didn't bring any western clothes with me, just suits," I responded. Mr. K stood up and shot back: *"Ridiculous! Take off your tie and come join us. You will have a great time! Rob, it was a pleasure to spend a few minutes with you. Thank you for your help and I look forward*

to sitting down again very soon. Roger, need anything else from me?" Roger replied: *"No sir. Thank you for your time."*

Mr. K shook my hand and he, Aaron, and Tony disappeared back through the door. Roger broke the silence with: *"Never a dull moment with Mr. K. That man is switched 'ON' twenty-four/seven. Do you have any questions, Rob?"* I responded with: *"Questions?! Are you kidding me? I am full of questions. The first one is, is he serious about the driver and a plane? Why would he do that? You guys have talent, way beyond what I can bring to the table. What can I offer that you don't already have? The cost of keeping a jet on stand-by for two or three days must be staggering. He doesn't take 'No' for an answer, does he?"*

Roger smiled and calmly addressed my questions by putting things into perspective for this thirty-one-year-old farm boy from central West Virginia. *"Do you remember when he said that he and Phil spoke while they were on the lake this weekend? Well, just to give you a feel for how Mr. K lives, that lake he is referring to is part of his Florida estate and is the largest privately owned lake in the state. I was on the yacht with him during Saturday's meeting with the users' board."* Roger continued: *"Don't think twice about the driver and the plane. With April and Aaron handling the arrangements, it is already done. In Mr. K's world, the car and the plane are a drop in the bucket. Clearly he has something in mind for you during that conference. Do you play chess, Rob?"* This struck me as an odd question and I responded with: *"Yes. I haven't played in a while, but I have always enjoyed a good game of chess."* *"Well Mr. K plays chess every day, on a global board, and he is very good at it. I can guarantee you that five or six months from now, we will know what was on his mind today. The guy is incredible. He sees things six, ten moves ahead and is usually right. On the other hand, he was dead serious when he said 'family first.' He expects nothing less than our best every day, but when our family needs us, Mr. K is the first to remind us that they are our top priority. Truly, you being here in April is up to you and Jennifer. I hope you can make it."*

"Now, regarding the party tonight, don't miss it. Mrs. K always organizes the best parties. Don't let what you are wearing keep you from missing out on

a great time. Shoot, the man himself told you to take off your tie and join us. I had some of the barbeque this weekend and it is excellent. Charlie Daniels is the entertainment and the fireworks after the show will be a sight to see. The hay wagons will start picking guests up at the front of the hotel at 6:30 this evening and they will bring you back whenever you are ready. Ish, we need to get to work. Rob, it was a pleasure to meet you and we look forward to working with you. Hope we can sit down for breakfast again in about six months." And with that, the meeting was over. Our waiter, knowing the important people had made their exit, asked me if I would be needing anything else. I assured him that I was finished and thanked him. With that, he removed the "reserved" plaque from the table and disappeared into what was now a sea of hungry conference goers.

I got up from the table, walked into the lobby, and made my way to the room where the first session of the day was to be held. The rest of the morning was uneventful. I did see Roger later that afternoon. I was out in the hall making my way to another session when I heard someone close to me say: *"Here is someone I would like for you to meet. Hey Rob. Do you have a minute?"* It was Roger with a group of three or four. He continued: *"Rob, let me introduce you to* (names of the people standing there) *the CEO, COO, and CIO of Southern Big Bank (SBB)."* Once again, I am using a fictional corporate name to represent a very large regional bank which was headquartered in Tennessee. Roger continued: *"SBB is considering upgrading their current system to K Corp. Gentlemen, Rob is with RB, Phil's bank. This is his first trip to K Corp's user conference. How has your morning gone so far, Rob?"* To which I replied: *"Great conference. RB is working with K Corp to leverage the technology for the benefit of the end user, creating point-of-sale platforms within each workstation, delivering more value to our customers. These folks are all focused on creating value for the customer, which makes for some very interesting conversations. Lots of new ideas."* SBB's CEO spoke up: *"That's what we are looking for! We want to put technology into the hands of our team members so they can better serve our customers. We are also looking at new ways to communicate with our board and shareholders. Sounds like we are in the right place."* At that point, we all shook hands and kept moving. I could tell from Roger's facial expressions that the brief conversation had gone well. Remember this chance encounter with the leadership team from SBB. This meeting, as seemingly random as it was, will become an important part of the next phase in my growth opportunities. It was just the next move in the ongoing chess match.

Later that evening, I took off my tie and headed to the barbeque. The hay wagons were each being pulled by a pair of the world-famous Budweiser Clydesdales. Unknown to me, there were, and I believe there still are, several teams of Clydesdales stabled all across the country. This particular team was stabled not far from Orlando. Beautiful horses! Massive animals with the kindest disposition. Nothing startled them. Truly, they were gentle giants.

I had just seen the hay wagon and already I was impressed. The remaining part of the evening did not disappoint. The setting, on the grounds of the World Center, was picture-perfect. The food was excellent and the entertainment was great. I ran into Mr. K that evening and he introduced me to his wife. I thanked them both for a wonderful evening and commented on the amount of work that must go into putting on a gathering like this one. Mr. K gave all the credit to his wife and, as I would learn in subsequent trips, she was truly the driving force behind organizing much of what took place at these conferences. She planned and oversaw every detail, from the headline entertainment down to the quality of the shuttle service. Now that I knew who she was, we would exchange pleasantries as we passed each other during these events. Whether it was 7:00 in the morning or 10:00 at night, Mrs. K was in constant motion, tending to every detail. She was a force to be respected and a remarkable individual. She was Ivy League educated, a recent Miss Florida, with high energy, and possessed a natural ability to communicate well with everyone. Together she and Mr. K made a formidable combination.

I was back in my room early that evening. At breakfast the next morning, some conference goers were commenting on the previous night's fireworks. I learned that I missed a spectacular display. The remaining couple of days at this conference were enjoyable and informative, but unremarkable when compared to that first day's events. The conference ended and I flew back to Columbus and drove home. Jennifer was there to greet me and all was right with the world.

The next five months passed quickly. Roger, Ish, several other K Corp team members, and I did spend a considerable amount of time working through system design and, most importantly, constructing a platform that would leverage the information contained within the software. Each time I was involved, the focus was not so much on programing and system architecture as it was on how to push the technology out to the POS, enhancing customer value. When you boiled all of these Orlando-based discussions down, my job was to keep the development team focused on the "Why," the purpose of the software's design. I served as the *keeper of the vision* for the K Corp group. What I came to realize was when Mr. K said that I was the "real deal" (implying that I somehow brought value to K Corp), he was talking about my ability to effectively communicate a clear vision and a clear purpose to all parties involved in this system re-design.

Herein lies one of the primary takeaways regarding the process of change. We will explore this critical point several times within these pages. There are always two differing cultures competing for the controlling influence over every form of change, regardless of how great or how small. Understanding these two cultures and the role they each play within the change process will make any leader much more effective when leading or managing the process of change.

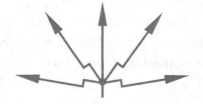

The Cultures of Change

Before I continue this series of life experiences, and relay the lessons learned from my trip to K Corp's technical conference, allow me to take a few minutes to introduce the two differing cultures of change. They are the culture of **DO** and the culture of **WHY**. See Illustration #1 below.

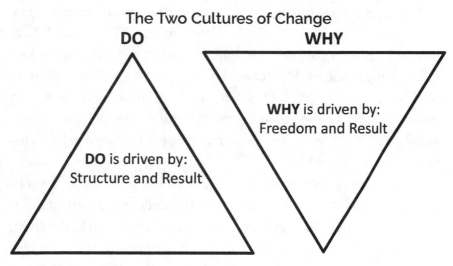

The Two Cultures of Change
DO   WHY

WHY is driven by:
Freedom and Result

DO is driven by:
Structure and Result

These two differing cultures exist in every relationship, corporate or personal, be it at the board table or the kitchen table. The reason these two cultures are found in every relationship is because they are always present when change is present and change, like time, is a constant in life. Because we all face change on a daily basis, many choose to deal with change by viewing it as an ally, a tool to be used to obtain a goal. Yet others see change as an enemy to be met head-on and defeated. The successful leader, the leader who learns to live better and lead differently, sees change not as an ally, nor as an enemy, but as a companion. It is a silent, ever-present partner in every relationship, a companion deserving of respect and understanding. We all learn to respect the power of change, usually through the wonderful lessons offered by failure. But, it would help us all if we had a better understanding of change and, for that, we need to learn about the cultures of change.

The cultures of DO and WHY can exist in their pure states, but only for finite periods of time. First, let's explore the culture of DO. By definition, **the culture of DO is one driven by structure and result**. The label of "DO" is what I have used to identify a culture represented by all of these examples: DO it; DO what you are told; DO as I say, not as I DO; DO not question me; Just get it DOne; DO it like we have always DOne it; etc. Notice that all of the examples of the culture of DO are closed-ended, non-inclusive statements. There is no further need for discussion, you just DO it.

> *The culture of DO is one driven by structure and result.*

The culture of DO, in its purest form, is the application of Maximum Command-And-Control (Max CAC) under the Terminal Leadership style (both of these references are from Book One). In this form, the culture of DO is so tightly structured that it holds total control over the population's access to the Cycle of Human Development. Think of this extreme as a population controlled by a ruthless dictator.

The vast majority of DO cultures exist to establish protective guidelines, a structure for the population to follow. This structure can take many forms, such as social norms, written laws, published regulations, established policies, acceptable procedures, etc. The structure established by the culture of DO provides a set of rules for managing change. If you learn and follow the established structure, you reduce the amount of risk. You will typically find the subject matter experts living and loving the environment within the culture of DO. Here, within this environment of structure, they will anchor their leadership platform for managing change.

The second culture found within the process of change is the culture of WHY. By definition, **the culture of WHY is driven by freedom and result**. The label of "WHY" is what I have used to identify a culture represented by all of these examples: WHY not; WHY can't we: WHY have or haven't we; WHY should or shouldn't we; WHY do or don't we; etc. Notice that all of these examples of WHY are open-ended, inclusive questions inviting further discussion and additional thought from the affected population.

> *The culture of WHY is driven by freedom and result.*

The culture of WHY, in its purest form, fosters maximum creativity under the very loose form of Transformational Leadership. It is a culture of pure creativity. Question everything. There are no restrictions placed on the population's access to the Cycle of Human Development. Think of this extreme in terms of four or five individuals living and working in the 1970s or 80s inside an old warehouse somewhere on the West Coast of the United States with no interior walls and no rules. A ping-pong table serves double duty as a workbench. At one end of the warehouse is a basketball rim and at the other end are the living quarters, a couple of worn-out couches, and a stack of empty pizza boxes. Personal hygiene is in short supply, but creative ideas abound. Out of this chaos comes the concepts which lead to the next Apple, Microsoft, or Google.

Creativity. The WHY culture is necessary to supply the process of change with its purpose. However, just like the extreme form of DO, WHY can only exist in an unchecked state for a limited time. Sooner or later, the next great idea will need financing, patent rights, sales contracts, etc. Structure, the culture of DO, the very thing that stifles creativity is now needed to enable the purpose of change to survive and grow.

And so, the process of change begins. The differing cultures of change cannot exist for an extended period without the strengths offered by the other. The chaos of creativity will always need structure to survive and structure, left unto itself, will always become overly restrictive without the renewed purpose offered by creativity.

Managing change, the structure of change, is typically done by the subject matter experts and, most often, they anchor their leadership platform within the culture of DO. Leading change, the purpose of change, is typically done by the thought leaders and risk takers. Change leaders typically anchor their leadership platforms within the culture of WHY. Those leading change will always be the first to position themselves so that they can better influence the process of change. This positioning, the **alignment** of the two cultures, is met, at first, with minimal resistance by those managing change. The subject matter experts thriving within the culture of DO will see the alignment as a distant curiosity. Within DO, there will exist a consensus that this new idea poses no immediate threat to the well-established status quo. Once the two cultures are in alignment (see Illustration #2 below), the leaders of change will begin to close the gap between DO and WHY through the increased use of substantive communication.

We know from our exploration of relationships in Book One and cultures in Book Two that increased substantive communication will tend to strengthen the relationship elements of trust and integrity. As a result, the leader will be granted enhanced influence over the culture which, by definition, is a collective relationship.

When the gap between the two cultures begins to narrow, resistance to the new purpose begins to build, creating friction. Friction, be it physical or emotional, creates heat or becomes a store of energy that is poised for future release. We have now begun to enter the next phase of the change process, which is termed the **Plate Tectonics of Change**.

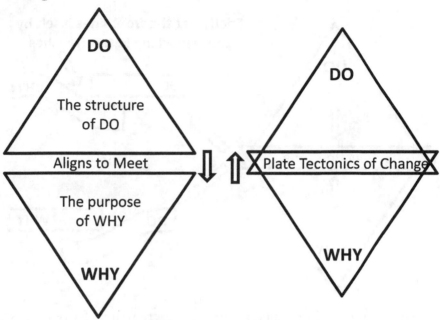

The Plate Tectonics of Change, like its geological namesake Plate Tectonics (the movement of large pieces of the Earth's crust) share many of the same characteristics. When the two cultures come into contact with each other, meaning when the leader of change (WHY) begins to force the new purpose onto the managers of change (DO), there will be a struggle for dominance. Friction between the two, structure and purpose, will build until one culture gains dominance over the other. Again, borrowing another descriptive term from the geological process, once dominance is established, there exists a subduction zone. Within the geological process, subduction occurs when the denser, heavier plate plunges beneath the lighter plate. The area where this subduction takes place is subject to intense earthquake activity and volcanic eruptions. The similarities between these two change processes, one geological and one cultural, are stunning.

Plate density within the geological model equates to cultural dominance within the change process model. At the point of contact, the cultural subduction zone, the dominate culture, will slide under the less dominate culture forming the foundation for change. See Illustration #3 below.

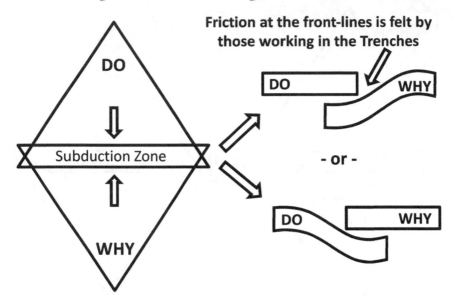

All along the cultural subduction zone, there will be friction/stress. On the surface, you will observe frequent eruptions in the form of emotional outbursts, terminations, resignations, promotions, the reassigning of key responsibilities, etc. In the corporate world, these eruptions can be observed within closed-door meetings, via updated organizational charts, and the occasional e-mail blast from the human resources department announcing changes in personnel. Cultural eruptions are significant in the moment, but once made public, their impact lessens. Over time, the cultures adjust to the eruption and all that remains is a new organizational landscape. However, cultural earthquakes, the second result of friction, are a completely different story.

Geological and culture earthquakes are both, by definition, the sudden release of stored energy which has been created by the collision of the two powerful forces. We understand the geological aspects of an earthquake, so let's explore the forces behind cultural earthquakes. During the process of change, the cultural store of energy begins when the less dominate culture chooses not to yield to the dominate culture. For example, assume the culture of WHY is the dominate culture and its new purpose forms the foundation of the change process. During the change process, there will be many times when the culture of DO will place existing structure (policy, procedure, accepted cultural norms, etc.) in the path of change, attempting to halt or delay its progression. In most instances, these attempts can be swept away by those leading change. But, there are always points in time where the structures placed in the path of change are formidable, causing friction to build between those forces leading change (WHY) and those forces managing change (DO). The more entrenched the resistance, the more the energy will build. Eventually, one culture will yield and the energy will be released. This release will be sudden and unpredicted, and the impact will be felt in all corners of the organization. There will be a resulting **Tsunami of Change** which will wash over the entire organization. Those leading change will do everything they can to avoid releasing a Tsunami of Change because, once released, the impact is uncontrollable. Rapid, massive change caused by a cultural earthquake, and the resulting tsunami will advance the new purpose, forcing the two cultures to expand their overlap. Unfortunately, once released, a Tsunami of Change can have the exact opposite effect, eroding the bond created by the new purpose, pushing the two cultures apart. If the two cultures are pushed apart, the leaders of change will announce that they are "pausing to reassess the strategic direction", and the managers of change will quietly celebrate their victory.

Here is where the geological and the cultural Plate Tectonic models differ. As the two cultures approach each other, skilled leaders of change will seek out a buffer, a cushion to be placed between the colliding cultures in order to relieve some the friction created by the process of change. This buffer can take many forms, but they fall into two very general categories, **objective buffers** and **subjective buffers**. Any type of buffer placed by the culture of WHY is used to help encourage and facilitate the change process. Any buffer put in place by the culture of DO will be used to strengthen the resistance against, or completely derail, the process of change.

Here are three very common examples of *objective (impartial) buffers* used by either culture to bolster their arguments for or against change. Regardless of the buffer's intended use, the end result from its application is less friction between the two cultures. The first and most commonly used objective buffer is the presentation of *new information* prepared in a compelling format and used to support the perspective held by one culture or the other. A second commonly used objective buffering technique is *manufacturing a threat* to the safety and security of the culture. Usually this threat manifests itself in the form of an enemy, a competitor, poised to do great harm to the organization if the proposed change is implemented or rejected, depending on your perspective. The third method of objective buffering is the application of *targeted financial rewards* used to incentivize the leaders and team members to strive toward a desired goal or produce a specific result.

Although these three objective buffers are effective in reducing friction, they usually pale in comparison to the effectiveness of a *subjective (biased) buffer*. The reason for the effectiveness of subjective buffers? Subjective buffers always take the form of an individual, a human catalyst, injected into the process of change in an effort to further either culture's objectives. In the struggle for dominance over the process of change, the use of individuals always trumps the leverage of new information or additional rewards.

Within the application of subjective buffers, there are two primary categories of human catalysts, external and internal. Let's start by discussing the most commonly used catalyst for change, the **external human catalysts (EHC)**. When you think of an EHC for change, what comes to mind? Most likely, your first thoughts go to the use of a third-party consultant, engaged by either culture, in support of their perspective regarding the proposed change. As you know, there is a massive, global industry which has developed around consulting in order to meet the ever-growing demand for subjective buffers. But, don't limit your thoughts to just "consultants."

External human catalysts come from a wide variety of third-party sources. There are all manner of external, subjective buffers available for use in the form of clergy, family, friends, lawyers, bankers, accountants, marriage counselors, teachers, coaches, etc. You get the idea. The selection of an EHC is driven primarily by the scope of the change process being proposed. Does one use subjective buffers in the form of external human catalysts at the board table or are they used for effecting change at the kitchen table? Answer: both. Also, keep in mind that EHCs are a critical part of the most challenging change process of all, changing the person we see in the mirror. Here is a truth that initially shocks most who hear it for the first time. The change process we are describing, the Plate Tectonics of Change and the use of objective and subjective buffers, is the same regardless of its application, whether on a group or an individual.

Take a moment and let that concept sink in. Whether you are changing a nation, a global corporation, a small business, a personal relationship, or yourself, the process of change is basically the same. Let's walk through it. First, identify the purpose (WHY) for change. Then align the new purpose with the existing structure (DO). Next, bring the purpose of change into contact with structure of change (alignment) using buffers to reduce the friction being produced from the process of change (Plate Tectonics of Change). A simple example would be the change process involved when you decide to lose a few pounds. Think through your experience using the change process terminology we have just outlined. With your newfound perspective, not only are you able to see how the process worked, but you can also see why the process succeeded or failed. Either result will yield you the opportunity to learn.

Now you know why this had to be a series of three books in order to help you to *LIVE better & LEAD differently*. Book One was written to help you better understand the "how" and "why" of relationships, be they with a collective or with self. Book Two was written to help you better understand the "how" and "why" of cultural transformation, the process of transforming behaviors within a culture (a collective relationship). We also discovered that the same processes used to transform a culture are successful when used to modify your own behaviors. Book Two simply took the concepts and models introduced in Book One and expanded on them. This book, Book Three, builds on the understanding gained from the first two books and provides the tools/ concepts necessary to apply what you have learned in order to effect lasting change. Interesting, isn't it? Each book can stand on its own, but from the beginning, the trilogy was designed to create a single, comprehensive experience for the reader. Collectively they form the how and why for effective leadership, be it leading a group or yourself.

My use of personal stories, actual Life Lessons learned along the way as a vehicle to deliver these concepts, is a unique delivery method. And, from the feedback I have received from many of you, this method has generated the desired result. The intent was to make the learning process personal to the reader. The objective was for you to attain a level of understanding well beyond the "what" and the "how." Personalizing these concepts is intended to help you better relate to the underlying "why." As you read about my Life Lessons, you will come to realize that you have your own set of life experiences from which you can glean understanding. The moment you personalize these concepts by relating them to your own experiences, you internalize the knowledge. Once internalized, the "how" and "why" from each book becomes a part of who you are as a leader, a parent, a partner, or a person. Each time you reapply one of these concepts, your skills will grow. These three books were not written for you just to read, but to LIVE. With each application, each experience, you will grow to live better as well as lead differently.

Whether dealing with the process of change in a group setting or individually, external human catalysts are helpful and, frequently, they are absolutely necessary. However, **internal human catalysts (IHCs)** are the most powerful enablers of change. By definition, an internal human catalyst resides within the relationship. The reason

IHCs are so effective is that they work in concert with the catalysts found within every relationship (emotion, purpose, and substance). Emotion, purpose, and substance are in constant motion within the structure of a relationship tending to the well-being of the relationship's three elements (trust, integrity, and communication). By definition, IHCs spend more time in direct contact with the change process than EHCs. Therefore, internal human catalysts have a greater opportunity to influence the result.

EHCs and IHCs both possess the ability to greatly influence, for better or worse, the results of change. What magical powers do EHCs and IHCs possess that are critical for maintaining a productive relationship and successfully facilitating the process of change? Answer: the power contained in their actions. There is no greater power within the process of change than the alignment of actions with words. And, the causes behind every individual's actions are human *choices* and *needs*.

Books One and Two explore human *choices* and *needs* in depth. Here, we will only list them and briefly summarize how they relate to internal buffers and the process of change. I do, however, encourage you to read more regarding these topics. *Choices* and *needs* are central themes within both Books One and Two.

There are four basic human *choices*: humility, curiosity, courage, and integrity. The first three are necessary in order for human growth to take place. With the addition of integrity, growth expands exponentially, enabling the individual to be granted a wide range of influence over others, and the granting of influence is the essence of leadership. Human *choice* is made, anew, every minute of every day. I may wake up one morning and choose to not be curious, but later that afternoon, something may catch my attention and I change my mind, becoming curious again. Each of the four *choices* are independent selections made by an individual or a population on a minute by minute basis. The sum total of our *choices* plays a major role in defining who we are as a person or as a group.

Others will observe our *choices* and use them to define our character and assess our strength of will. Over time, the more consistent we are in making our *choices*, the more those around us can accurately predict our responses. When others gain confidence in their ability to predict our behavior, they grant us an enhanced level of trust. Earning trust and choosing integrity both work to enhance the effectiveness of any human catalyst which, in turn, further enables the process of change through the reduction of friction between the two opposing cultures. Based on the consistency of their actions, both cultures can perceive the catalyst as someone with which they can work, someone they can trust.

Working in tandem with the *choices* we all make are the basic human *needs* we all possess. There are four basic human *needs*: safety, security, purpose, and love. As is true with *choice*, the first three are necessary in order for human growth to take place. With the addition of the fourth *need*, love (the verb love), individual growth expands exponentially. Developing the *need* to love drives a leader to seek influence over others in an effort to help them attain their legitimate *needs*.

Unlike human *choices*, human *needs* are sequential and interdependent. If my need for safety is unmet, I cannot feel secure. If I am safe but my perception of long-term safety is uncertain, I will have no need for a different set of actions until I achieve security. Once safety and security have been attained, I have a foundation from which I can seek new purpose. For example, let's say that in the pursuit of a new job (a new purpose), there is a question raised by my immediate supervisor regarding my future employment, as when the CFO threatened my continued employment at RB. The natural human instinct would be to regress, to pull back from current behaviors in order to focus on my *need* for security. However, an individual who has grown to a point where they have developed a sense of self-directed purpose has attained a permanent foundation for continued growth, barring the impact of unforeseen disasters (accident, sudden illness, etc.). Leaders who obtain self-directed purpose are viewed as confident, mature, and forward-looking. Leaders who obtain the next level of *need*, love, are viewed in the same terms as leaders with self-directed purpose plus these additional attributes: compassionate, inspirational, and visionary.

An EHC or IHC at work within any relationship possessing humility, curiosity, courage, integrity, and a self-direct purpose will become a formidable force for change. If one of the competing cultures within the process of change harnesses such a catalyst, and combines it with a series of supporting objective buffers, their cultural goals would most likely be accomplished. Within the subduction zone, all of these factors: purpose, structure, buffers, and catalysts combine to affect the process of change.

The struggle for control over the process of change occurs within the subduction zone, at the point of first contact between structure and purpose. If the culture of DO (structure) is perceived as the most credible and strongest force, then it will slide underneath the culture of WHY (purpose) and form the foundation of the change process. A foundation formed by the culture of DO will force the new purpose to conform to the existing structure. The result from this outcome will likely be incremental change, small steps forward at best.

However, if the culture of WHY (purpose) is seen as the most credible and strongest force for change, then it will slide underneath the culture of DO (structure) and form the foundation of the process. A foundation formed by the culture of WHY will force the existing structure to alter itself in order to accommodate the new purpose. This outcome is commonly termed reengineering, or innovation, resulting in radical leaps forward.

Just as a point of interest, do you know what the geological term is for the point where one Tectonic Plate slides under another? Answer: a trench. Ocean trenches are some of the deepest locations on earth. Trench regions possess massive pressure levels and, until recently, have been assumed to be void of life. However, recently developed technologies have enabled explorers to go to the deepest parts of the oceans and, much to their surprise, they have discovered the trenches to be teaming with life. Do you know where the most crucial work will be done during any change process? Answer: in the trenches, which are teaming with employees and customers. What a coincidence!

All of our discussions up to this point have centered on those leading change, those driving the culture of WHY (purpose), and those managing change while driving the culture of DO (structure). Now it is time to shift our focus to those living and working within the trenches of change. If you want a change process to result in successful, lasting innovation, the most important people are those actually performing change management. **Change management** is performed by three basic groups of people: those who are actually doing the work, those who are leading those who actually do the work, and the human catalysts, external and internal. You will always find these three groups of people in the trenches and working throughout the entire subduction zone. What do these three groups do that makes them so valuable? These are the folks that receive the new purpose from the culture of WHY, along with the resulting changes to structure from the culture of DO. Change managers are the ones who reshape the culture's purpose/structure in order to deliver real, tangible value to the organization's end users and their customers. Bear in mind that those working at these organizational depths usually have very little light (a lack of communication). They are also under tremendous pressures, pressure from dealing eye to eye with the customer, in addition to dealing with the expectations levied on them from those occupying the organizational boxes above them.

> *Change managers are the ones who reshape the culture's purpose/structure in order to deliver real, tangible value to the organization's end users and their customers.*

Change management is the process of making change actually work. Change management is the process of determining the organization's or individual's **capacity** for change. Those employees working in the trenches (on the front lines), their direct supervisors, and the related human catalysts hold the keys to change management. These three groups will make or break the process of change, regardless of the culture ultimately forming the foundation.

By the time the real work begins, actually implementing the process of change, the wisdom offered by the external human catalysts has become a distant memory. If the EHC was a consultant for DO or WHY, the conclusions reached and the recommendations offered are typically neatly organized in a three-ring binder or they reside on a thumb drive. The binders can be found sitting on a shelf collecting dust in the sponsoring executive's office. If the information is on a thumb drive, it will be laying in a forgotten corner of a desk drawer within the same office. In most circumstances, when the rubber meets the road and change is actually being implemented, it will be the result of the internal human catalysts working in the trenches with the remaining change managers. Front line employees, front line leaders, and IHCs are left to ultimately make the process work by figuring out how to balance what is being demanded with what is possible. The ability to balance what is wanted with what is possible serves as the definition of **capacity** within the process of change.

> *The ability to balance what is wanted with what is possible serves as the definition of capacity within the process of change.*

The key to increasing the capacity for change is the effective use of substantive communication. Those tasked with leading change know that substantive communication must take place at all levels of the organization and especially within the levels that will become the trenches and subduction zones of change. The more frequent and transparent the communication, the more weight (importance) assigned to the purpose (the WHY). As the two cultures move into closer proximity and contact actually occurs and if the leaders of change have failed to effectively communicate purpose, the managers of change will fill the vacuum created by the lack of information. Those managing change will fill the vacuum by frequently stressing the threats being posed to the existing structure via the new change. Through the use of buffers and catalysts, they will inject just enough fear into the new purpose to sow the seeds of doubt.

The culture that effectively communicates in advance with those in charge of capacity will successfully form the foundation for change. The bottom line is, as the two cultures collide, whichever culture has most effectively influenced those in charge of change management will ultimately impose their will over the process of change.

Over my career, especially the most recent ten years, I have had the opportunity to help turn around and grow a few companies in various industries. During this period, I have frequently found myself leading change, managing change, and performing change management all at the same time. This is very often the case in a turnaround environment, especially when working with smaller companies (under $100 million in annual revenues). Early on, I developed the following guidelines to help me stay focused on the mission.

My focus is always on **risk, capacity, and opportunity**. Risk, capacity, and opportunity are three keys to understanding the process of change. From the moment I walk into a company (a division, department, or a one-on-one with an executive), these guidelines apply. Two of these three key elements are very familiar to leaders and managers. Risk, in all of its forms (financial, operational, legal, reputational, political, cultural, etc.) is always front and center for managers when evaluating change. Because it is familiar to us all, there is very little I need to add regarding risk. The second element, the element which is always top of mind for leaders, is opportunity. Where the structure of risk is usually well established, the element of opportunity is frequently wide open, limited only by the experience and creativity of the leader. Does this all sound familiar? DO will focus on the risks and WHY will focus on the opportunities. Think back to our earlier discussion when we introduced the concepts of the two cultures. The culture of DO is one of structure and results. The culture of DO exists to manage/mitigate risk in all of its forms through establishing structure in order to enhance results. The culture of WHY is one of freedom and results. The culture of WHY exists to encourage the perception of opportunity by maintaining the freedom to innovate.

Sandwiched between the two well-known keys to change, risk and opportunity, lies the lesser known, but perhaps the most important key, capacity. We now know that successful change management requires a clear-eyed view of what is wanted, balanced against what is possible. When balancing the process of change, always prioritize your thoughts under risk, capacity, and opportunity.

When you consider all we have learned so far about the process of change, it becomes clear as to why I chose to share these particular stories about my life experiences with RB, K Corp, and SBB. Let's recap what we have covered in the stories and tie the experiences directly back to these leadership models by moving forward in our journey, *Orlando in April.*

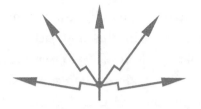

Orlando in April

We opened the story by covering the meeting with all the RB executive team. This was the meeting held to decide on whether or not RB would pursue the opportunity offered by establishing the first ATM network in our market. Place this meeting into context by using the concepts around the cultures of WHY and DO and keeping in mind what you now know about the process of change. Outside of the CEO, the EVP of trust and investment, and myself, all those seated at the table were card-carrying members of the culture of DO. As a group, their focus was squarely on risk mitigation, which would be accomplished by maintaining RB's existing structures. This was the group focused on managing change. They leveraged consensus during this meeting to present a strong and united front in opposition to any new purpose.

The CEO was the only openly supportive member within the culture of WHY. Mr. E saw the storm clouds gathering on the horizon and saw an opportunity for RB. His vision was to protect RB's market share by leveraging technology and pushing information out to the end users, the POS, in an effort to enhance customer value. He saw establishing an ATM network as a good first step in the process of change. Mr. E was leading change. He was the keeper of the vision and the lone advocate at the table for the new purpose.

Given the level of emotion present at the table that day, one can assume the opposing cultures had already been aligned, which was indeed the case. Not only were the cultures aligned, but they were moving into close proximity, which explains the subsequent eruptions by the CFO. Working on behalf of the culture of WHY, serving as a subjective buffer, was K Corp. Mr. K was actually serving as an external human catalyst within this process, sharing and even helping to create the vision of opportunity held by Mr. E, as well as the vision held by SBB's CEO. Keep in mind that the process of change is equivalent to the game of chess being played on three or four different levels. Those that develop a skill for successfully implementing change have developed the ability to see six moves ahead in the game on many different levels (witness Mr. K's considerable success in the highly competitive IT industry).

When I raised my hand and responded to Mr. E's invitation for other thoughts, I marked myself as a target of both cultures. The culture of DO wanted me to conform to the defined, existing RB structure. The CFO's task was to force me into conformity or move me out of the organization. I had also unknowingly marked myself as a potential internal human catalyst for the culture of WHY and, as such, I posed a threat to the status quo. Mr. E, the lone member of the culture of WHY, targeted me as well. His mission was to explore my strengths and weaknesses as a potential internal human catalyst working on behalf of WHY.

Notice the drastic differences between the initial meetings held immediately after I unknowingly inserted myself into the middle of the RB cultural battle. Mr. E's first meeting with me was focused on better understanding my choices, evaluating my character. John's first meeting with me was centered on manipulation through fear and intimidation in order to force my compliance with the existing culture of DO. Both men gained a clear understanding of my character during the course of these first meetings. My future at RB came down to one seeing potential where the other saw a problem. As time passed, representatives from both cultures tested my character and my resolve. When the lines were finally drawn, I had become a change manager for the culture of WHY.

By now, it was the first part of April. The door on the plane closed and the jet was pushed back from the terminal. I was leaving Columbus, Ohio, and headed to Orlando, Florida, for my second trip. This time, I was the only RB representative that would be attending the conference. Our *new* CIO had just been hired and did not have his feet on the ground firmly enough yet to be making this trip to Orlando. This time, as the jet taxied to get in line for takeoff, my mind was not on what opportunities may lie ahead, but rather on what I had left behind. Jennifer was eight months pregnant. Things had been pretty uneventful for the last few months, but we were getting close to the big event. The last thing I wanted to do was to hop on a plane and fly off to another conference. But, Jennifer was perfectly fine with me being away for a couple of days and her parents were only a few hundred yards down the street, if needed. My actually being there on the ground at the conference was seemingly very important to both Mr. E and Mr. K. The engines roared to life and a couple hours later, I was on the monorail at the Orlando airport in hopes to find my luggage waiting for me in the other terminal. I pulled my luggage off the conveyer belt, boarded onto the waiting shuttle, and headed to the World Center. The quicker we get this thing started, the faster I can get back home.

Allow me to fill in some missing pieces. Mr. K had been more than good to his word. In the event of an emergency, April and Robin had me covered six ways to Sunday. I had complete contact information for April, Aaron, a driver, the pilot, and Mrs. K (Mr. K was going to be out of the country during this conference). As I registered at the front desk, the clerk provided me with a packet of information for the conference. Included in the packet were additional copies of the "contact in case of an emergency" information. In addition, and at the request of Mrs. K, the hotel had extended the hours of their black car service to cover any gaps in the coverage that may exist with the contracted limo service. The car, my car, was parked just outside the main entrance to the resort's lobby.

The clerk also passed on a couple of messages from Mrs. K. First, she welcomed me to the conference and expressed again that she and Mr.

K were grateful that I was able to attend. Then, she added a personal touch when the clerk passed on the second message. Mrs. K had sent word to remind me to call Jennifer as soon as I got into the room and to call her as many times as I wished during the conference. The hostess then reminded me that the room, all related charges, my meals at the World Center, and all transportation services were compliments of Mr. and Mrs. K and the World Center.

My thirty-one-year-old self was impressed with all the time, trouble, and expense that they had gone through in order to meet my personal requirements. K Corp had gone through all of this just so I would attend this particular conference. But, as thoughtful as everyone had been, my thoughts remained on the same question that had plagued me since that breakfast meeting with Mr. K, Roger, and Ish five months ago, "Why?" More specifically: "Why me?"

I was not a power player in a large bank and I certainly wasn't a resource for technical advice. K Corp had some of the best and brightest programmers and system engineers in the world. No, the reasons behind the value they had assigned to my attending this conference were still unknown. I thought of something Roger had said during the breakfast meeting five months ago. This was an ongoing game of chess. There was a strategy at work here which had yet to reveal itself. I had made my move. I was in Orlando in April, as requested. Now, it was someone else's move. I assumed the person controlling the pieces on the other side of the board was Mr. K. All I could do now was to wait for him to make the next move.

That evening and the next morning's breakfast were uneventful. The first two sessions I attended went as expected, nothing new. There were about twenty to thirty people in attendance at each of these first two sessions. My third session began midmorning, and according to the agenda, the session was to be led by Roger. As I walked into this third session, the setting was very different from my first two meetings. The room was large. I would guess it held about two hundred people and, from the looks of it, every seat was going to be filled. This session was scheduled to last for two hours, so as was my custom, I found a seat near the back of the room and settled in. Roger stepped to the podium and began the session. The topic that had captured the attention of so many attendees was related to K Corp's leveraging of the information generated by their latest software version. More specifically, people were interested in "what" and "how" K Corp was going to deliver this information into the hands of the end users. This was going to be a very interesting session. Roger, his team, and I had spent a bunch of time over the last several months on this topic. I was very curious as to which ideas had actually been incorporated into the final version of the software.

As Roger spoke, I was pleased to hear that many of the concepts we had worked on together had actually made it into the final product. As he continued with his remarks, Roger told the assembled group that many of these concepts had been developed by K Corp's customers. He stressed that K Corp understood the importance of listening and responding to the needs of their customers, much like we (the banks) responded to the needs of our customers. The goal of K Corp was to deliver enhanced value to their users by not just focusing on the "How" of information delivery, but rather K Corp was focused on the "Why" behind the information. K Corp had spent this last few months not so much writing code, but rather developing a new purpose for the information being captured within their system. The next move in the chess match was about to be made.

Roger paused briefly and then said: *"As I said earlier, much of the purpose, the application of the new system's information, came directly from our customers. I want to recognize one customer in particular for their role in the development of this latest version. Rob Walters with RB, are you here this morning?"* From my seat in the back of the room, I raised my hand. (Seems like this whole thing started with my raising my hand and here I was doing it again.) Roger continued: *"There he is, clear in the back. Rob, I haven't had a chance to talk with you this morning, but would you be willing to come up here and share with the group your vision of why this new software will deliver enhanced value to RB and its customers?"* What was I going to say, no? I replied: *"Good morning, Roger. Sure, if you would like. I would be glad to share with the group what we have been working on."* Roger encouraged the group to take a ten-minute break while they got me wired up.

When I reached the front of the room, they hooked me up to a mic. Roger and I spent a couple minutes planning the format of the discussion. He wanted to do a question and answer session between the two of us, then open it up to the audience for questions. As we were about to resume the session, I leaned over and asked Roger: *"Are we playing chess?"* Roger came back with a quick smile and a nod, acknowledging that the game was in progress. At this point, I couldn't even see the board, much less the pieces being moved. I was truly just along for the ride. Oh well, no risk, no gain. The topics Roger and I discussed were very familiar and covered the development process from the prior five months. When we opened it up to the audience for their comments or questions, there was an immediate response from several attendees. Our Q&A lasted about thirty minutes and went smoothly. After the session, I remained seated up front as Roger brought the session to a close.

"Did we accomplish what we needed to accomplish?" I asked Roger as the guests were filing out. In a hushed tone, Roger responded, *"Not yet, but I think we are about to…."* Roger interrupted himself and walked to the edge of the platform to greet a couple of gentleman that had been in the audience. After a brief conversation with them, Roger motioned me over to join the group. He introduced the gentlemen as the CFO and controller for SBB. These two were executives with SBB, the same bank holding company as the CEO, COO, and CIO I had briefly met during the conference in October. The CFO spoke up, *"Good morning, Rob. Our CEO asked me to look you up during this conference. Do you have plans for lunch?"* I returned the greeting and replied: *"No plans, gentlemen, and I am ready to eat. Let's go find a sandwich. Roger, do you have time to join us."* Roger answered with: *"No thank you, not today. I need to get back to the office for a conference call with Keith. Thanks for your help today, Rob."*

With that being said, we all shook hands with Roger and the SBB execs and I headed to lunch. The large wooden double doors to the meeting room closed behind us. I didn't know it at the time, but those doors closing behind me would come to symbolize the transitioning of my role within RB. There was going to be an opportunity offered over lunch that would change the course of my RB career. I was finally going to get a glimpse of the chess board which would help me to better understand the "Why" behind all of this fuss over my attending this particular conference.

That was the last time I would see Roger face to face. He and I would speak often over the next few months as events related to SBB would unfold. However, change being the constant that it is, my duties at RB would expand rapidly within the next year, as would Roger's responsibilities within K Corp. Roger went on to assume a leadership role for K Corp in Eastern Europe. I, on the other hand, was about to begin a journey toward what would become my future. That morning, the doors had closed on whatever opportunities that may have laid ahead for me in the world of system design and application. However, the double doors leading into the restaurant were propped wide open. Let's eat lunch!

The two SBB executives and I found a table suitable for discussing business inside one of the restaurants within the World Center complex. The meeting went as these meetings typically go. We got to know each other a little better by exchanging verbal resumes and personal histories (family, interests outside of work, etc.). After we ordered lunch, the SBB executives got down to business. They proposed an exchange of what amounted to my knowledge/experience of applying the information within the new K Corp software. In turn, I would be able to spend some time observing the inside workings of their merger and acquisition (M&A) process.

SBB was proposing that I come to their headquarters in Tennessee for three days and work with their management information team. The first of these exchanges between RB and SBB would take place within the next few months. They proposed two three-day trips, with the first being in July or August. The follow-up trip would be scheduled a couple months later. Before I could even pose the question, the CFO assured me that our respective CEOs had discussed and approved the exchange, pending the results of our meetings during this conference. I also learned that Mr. K had been involved in a series of behind-the-scenes discussions with SBB's and RB's CEOs. My part in the chess match was becoming clearer. I began to see who was moving the pieces and I could guess at the possible strategy being employed. I would go on to learn that discussions had been ongoing since the user conference in October. At that time, when I briefly met the CEO, SBB was deciding on which software company to choose for their future growth. Ultimately, their decision to purchase the K Corp software was driven by the application concepts being developed by Roger and his team.

The goal was for me to assist SBB's management information team to leverage (apply) the technology and information contained within this latest version of K Corp's software, ultimately delivering enhanced value to SBB's end users. SBB saw the strategic advantage in implementing the same type of point-of-service concepts that Mr. E had been working on at RB. Basically, they wanted to take what Roger and I had been talking about in the prior session and implement it within the markets SBB served. In exchange for my time, SBB would pay my expenses plus, and this is the important part, they would arrange for me to spend time during these trips working with their M&A team. Bingo! Done deal. I will explain why the M&A piece was so important later when we resume our journey through this experience and when I summarize my trip to SBB. But for now, we need to pause the story just long enough to retrace the movement of the chess pieces that had led up to this point.

This all began when Mr. K first introduced his vision of enhanced POS/customer value to K Corp's user board. Mr. E was the only member of the user board that openly supported the concept. Actually, he had latched on to the concept immediately. Mr. E understood that the vision being laid out by Mr. K was exactly what RB needed to differentiate itself from its future competitors. Here is how this played out from Mr. E's perspective. His vision was not focused on the current state of RB's performance, but on the future state of our ability to profitably compete with much larger banks for our customers' business. He understood that the dark storm clouds that were gathering on the horizon represented significant increases in both federal and state banking regulations, which would result in reduced profits for RB. At the same time, profits were being reduced, RB would be forced to incur significantly more expenses to support state and federally mandated back room operations (accounting, audit, SEC and FDIC compliance, etc.). In this future state, Mr. E believed that smaller banks like RB would be under ever-increasing pressure to generate growth to maintain profit margins in order to satisfy the future demands from our customers and shareholders.

Mr. E understood that for RB to meet future customer and shareholder demands, we needed to develop a competitive edge. We needed a method of delivering enhanced value to our customers by becoming more efficient and effective at delivering our financial services. If we failed to achieve this level of fundamental change, he was convinced that RB's return to shareholders would suffer, and we would begin losing market share to the much larger banks. Mr. E anticipated that the bigger banks would enter our markets through the process of gobbling up the smaller banks via acquisition. His vision of the future was clear and it proved to be very accurate.

Now enters SBB into the mix. Through his never-ending marketing efforts, Mr. K discovered that he, Mr. E, and the chairman of the board of directors for SBB, a potential new customer, all shared the same vision. All three leaders foresaw significant changes looming on the horizon within the financial services industry. Mr. K saw these changes as a huge business opportunity. He knew that if K Corp could develop a product which integrated the newest mainframe computer platform with the rapidly growing use of personal computers, they

would leap even further ahead of their competitors. I know it is difficult to imagine, but at this point in time, the personal computer was
very limited in its capacity and application. This was the age of floppy
disks and monochrome CRTs. What was being proposed by K Corp
was a radical concept for its time and would advance the application
of available technologies well beyond what was currently being done.
The stakes for K Corp were very high, but that is how Mr. K had successfully built his company. He was a visionary and a risk taker.

The chairman of SBB was also a visionary. Like Mr. E, he too saw
the storm clouds of change gathering on the horizon and understood
their implications to the financial services industry. However, SBB's
chairman perceived the coming changes from a completely different
perspective. Mr. E's view was a perspective held by a much smaller
bank, seeking to protect its market share from the invasion of the bigger
banks. SBB had already achieved "bigger bank" status. SBB's chairman
saw the opportunity as one that would help them to rapidly grow market share in new and existing markets. SBB intended to leverage the
coming changes by entering new markets through acquisitions. Their
mission was to apply K Corp's new software in the exact same manner
as RB, putting more information in the hands of the end users at the
POS. SBB's and RB's goals were identical; deliver enhanced value to
the customer. SBB saw this competitive advantage, combined with the
considerable value associated with owning SBB's stock, as an opportunity to further accelerate their already aggressive expansion plans. They
planned to expand through the purchase of existing, smaller banks.

On the surface, one may think that RB and SBB should have been
uncooperative competitors. Clearly, each was seeking a competitive
advantage within their respective markets. The leaders of the two
companies shared the same vision regarding the future of financial
services, but they perceived the resulting opportunities from polar
opposite perspectives. It may not seem logical, but cooperation
between those holding opposing strategic views represents the normal
environment when effectively dealing with the process of change.

What was unique about this life experience was I was dealing with three strong and successful leaders of change who all shared a common purpose.

Have you heard the old phrase: "we are dealing with two sides of the same coin"? That small bit of wisdom is an excellent way to summarize what was taking place between RB, SBB, and K Corp. Those of you who have read Books One and Two know that I always strive to use tangible illustrations so other leaders can better understand intangible concepts. The coin works well in this instance. The coin represents an identifiable process of change. In this case, the storm clouds on the horizon represent pending regulatory changes to the way the financial services industry conducted its core businesses. Each side of the coin represents opposing or opposite perspectives regarding the perceived risks and opportunities being presented by the process of change. The leaders of RB and SBB saw the same clouds and agreed on the application of the same strategic solution to mitigate future risks and capitalize on the market opportunities. The common strategic solution was to be facilitated by Mr. K's development of new software.

In keeping with our illustration, on one side of the coin Mr. E wanted to protect RB's existing market share by better serving his customer base. On the other side of the coin, SBB's chairman wanted to continue to expand his share of existing markets, while entering into new markets, all of which would be accomplished by better serving his customer base. And what did the third party in this change process, Mr. K, expect to gain out of this process of change? Answer: the coin itself (figuratively and literally). K Corp expected to be rewarded for Mr. K's vision, creativity, and willingness to accept the high level of business risk. He had already invested considerable resources in developing the new software. Mr. K had seen the storm clouds gathering long before RB and SBB. He recognized the pending change, discovered the opportunity buried within, evaluated the risks, and invested his resources to design a solution to a problem that didn't even exist yet. In a word, Mr. K's risk and reward were centered on **innovation**.

Mr. K and K Corp owned the rights to the coin (they owned the results from their innovation), for better or worse, because they were willing to accept the risks. RB and SBB also owned the results from their application of K Corp's innovative solution. These three leaders were each skilled, in their own way, at perceiving the opportunities buried within every change process. Multiple times within Books One and Two, we referenced the power contained within perception, a perspective which was expressed as *holding the issue up to the light*. This series of events is yet another example of the awesome power of understanding.

Improved understanding is available to any leader that learns to view change from multiple perspectives at the same time. Learn to *see the duck from both the shore and from under the water at the same time* (another familiar reference from Books One and Two). When you learn to simultaneously view an issue from multiple perspectives, you will have acquired the ability to anticipate the future, enabling you to see around the corner. You will never be 100 percent correct in your anticipation of future events, but in time, your percentages with improve. Shoot, a professional baseball player that gets a hit four times for every ten times at bat is worthy of celebration. Anticipating the future, especially when individuals are involved, is certainly much more complex than hitting a baseball. The key to successfully anticipating a curve ball or predicting a change in the financial services industry is practice, followed by experience, followed by more practice (the Cycle of Human Development).

> *When you learn to simultaneously view an issue from multiple perspectives, you will have acquired the ability to anticipate the future, enabling you to see around the corner.*

If Mr. K, Mr. E, and SBB's chairman were each the driving force behind the purpose of change, leading their respective cultures of

WHY, who was managing the change process within these organizations? Who represented the cultures of DO, the structure of change? Good questions and here are the answers.

Within K Corp, Roger, Ish, and several others within the software development team definitely provided the structure of change. But, within K Corp, as long as Mr. K was supporting it, the culture of WHY was always going to be the denser plate, forming the foundation for structure when the two cultures of change collided.

Within RB, the executive leadership team formed the culture of DO, providing the structure to Mr. E's purpose. In recent years, consensus among the members of RB's culture of DO had successfully throttled the process of change down to one of incremental improvements only. RB's executive team had created an environment of manageable changes resulting in minimal risk. A primary example of the mindset and the strength of DO within RB would be the results of the discussion regarding the creation of the first ATM network in our markets.

I didn't know it at the time, but SBB's culture of DO was currently the dominate force within their organization. The SBB executive team, led by their current CEO, managed change by implementing structure at every turn. As with RB, SBB's executive leadership team managed all change through consensus, which had the same definition in both companies, meaning uniformed compliance with the imposed structure. SBB's CEO was a member, in good standing, within the culture of DO. The real keeper of the vision, the driving force behind SBB's purpose, was their chairman, who had served as SBB's CEO for many years before semi-retiring from that position. I would later learn that almost all of SBB's growth to national prominence within their peer group (banks with assets greater than $5 billion, but less than $10 billion), occurred under the leadership of the previous CEO, their current chairman.

Given what we have learned about the process of change so far, we can predict with a pretty high degree of confidence which of these three companies will be the most successful in implementing the new purpose. Since we have the advantage afforded by twenty-twenty hindsight, we don't have to wonder about the outcomes. K Corp and RB were successful in implementing this particular process of change. In both cases, purpose drove structure. Purpose formed the foundation and the results were innovative, with major leaps forward in generating enhanced customer and shareholder value.

Within SBB, structure would form the foundation for this change. When the two cultures came into contact, and the time came to implement change, the culture of DO was the denser of the two, sliding under the culture of WHY. Within SBB, structure would drive purpose and the opportunity to leap forward in a highly competitive market would be limited. SBB would implement change, but with structure driving purpose, only incremental improvements would be realized.

"How did the three organizations utilize buffers?" you ask. A great question and here is your answer. All three organizations utilized objective buffers (presenting new information, identifying threats to safety and security, and targeting financial rewards) to varying degrees. All three also applied subjective buffers (external and internal human catalysts) in an effort to reduce the friction caused by change. But, here is a key trend you will find present in almost all change processes. When the culture of DO forms the foundation for change, the vast majority of the influence within the subduction zone will come from objective buffers, with some use of external human catalysts. The opposite is true when the culture of WHY forms the foundation for change. When purpose forms the foundation for change, the vast majority of the influence within the subduction zone will come from subjective buffers and they rely heavily on the use of internal human catalysts.

Going back to the three organizations, I would become the lead IHC for change within RB's process. My role as an internal catalyst for change within RB would last for a few years. During this period, I became RB's lead change manager. The process for change, the leveraging of technology, would eventually be replaced by RB's focus on growth through the mergers and acquisitions. My focus on M&A

would go on to be replaced by RB's need for an educational program which was designed to generate growth within the board and the executive leadership team. I had become a force for purpose, competing with the culture of DO to affect the process of change. After leading several battles where purpose won over structure, I would eventually lose to the forces of DO, but that is another story for another time.

I was on loan to K Corp from RB to act as a temporary IHC within their subduction zone. In both examples of successful change, my role as an internal catalyst came with the full and open support of the change leaders (Mr. K and Mr. E). The support of the CEO of an organization doesn't guarantee the effectiveness of an IHC, but it sure helps. Much of my success or failure as an IHC was dependent on my own strength of character and maturity as a leader. However, an internal catalyst without the full and unwavering support of the change leader(s) is guaranteed to fail. The key to my ability to successfully help K Corp was rooted in the strength of the relationship between Mr. K and Mr. E. Recalling the Relationship Model (Book One), the trust, integrity, and communication which existed between the two CEOs formed the relationship which granted me influence within K Corp's subduction zone. However, when it came to my work with SBB, I did not have the benefit of a productive relationship, which would make my duties as an IHC more difficult. Speaking of SBB, let's get back to lunch!

Armed with the knowledge of why and how the process of change works, and with a more complete understanding of what was happening behind the scenes as the chess pieces were being moved, let's continue with our story. SBB's CFO, controller, and I were meeting over lunch after the conclusion of a late morning session in which Roger and I conducted a Q & A on the topic of K Corp's new software release. The executives from SBB wanted to continue the discussion over lunch, but Roger had prior commitments and could not join us. While seated in one of the restaurants within the Orlando World Center, the SBB CFO and controller proposed an exchange of knowledge between RB and SBB. The exchange being proposed had already been approved by the respective CEOs of the two bank holding companies, with the knowledge and assistance of Mr. K.

Here is how this exchange was envisioned to work. I would fly to SBB's headquarters in Tennessee and work with their management information team. My side of the exchange was to help them harness the mountains of newly available information within the most recent software update. In exchange, I was to spend a period of time learning from SBB's M&A team, which had gained a national reputation for its skill. This exchange was to take place during two trips to SBB's headquarters, one in July or August and the second will take place a couple months later.

One half-eaten club sandwich later, the deal was struck. The three of us exchanged contact information and shook hands. The rest of K Corp's technical conference was uneventful. I never used the car that Mr. K had arranged, nor did I have need of the corporate jet that they had placed on stand-by. Jennifer and I were blessed with the birth of our son in the latter part of May and the rest, as they say, is history.

On my return to RB, I met with Mr. E several times to discuss the events from the conference. He was very insistent on my learning all that I could about SBB, their history, their operations, and especially their M&A process. SBB's reputation for the frequent and successful acquisition of smaller banks had gained them national recognition. They had developed their M&A process into a very effective tool for expanding market presence and enhancing shareholder value. Now that RB had begun implementing the process of leveraging technology, pushing information out to the POS, Mr. E was ready to begin the next step in his vision for RB to survive the storm clouds.

The next step in what turned out to be a three-step evolution for RB was to build our own M&A process. Our process was to be constructed using what we knew about our markets, combined with what I could learn from SBB's process. With my backgrounds in leadership, sales, accounting, and banking, Mr. E saw me as not only the internal catalyst for buffering the current change process, but he also saw me as the person to lead RB's M&A initiative. There was much more to learn.

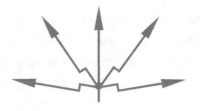

Tennessee in July

It was late July, and it was hot when the plane accelerated down the runway. Two flights and a rental car later, I was checking into a hotel that was just across the street from SBB's headquarters. Unlike my experience in working with Roger's team, I had heard very little from the CFO and controller in preparation for my being on site. The next morning, I worked my way through SBB's security and visitor protocols. In short order, I found myself waiting in a lobby for the better part of an hour, before someone from the management information team came down to escort me up to their floor. The building itself was impressive, inside and out. The external design of SBB's headquarters, the furniture and internal appointments, the look and attitude of the people, and the entire atmosphere projected success and prestige.

The management information team was located on the same floor as the CEO, CFO, the boardroom, and several other c-suite offices. Believe me, they spared no expense in creating the work environments on this floor. I noticed the finest in furnishings with the latest in technology, all on display within a spacious and elegant floor plan. I was politely escorted to a small, but very comfortable conference room located in the back corner of the building. Coffee, juice, fruit, and pastries were all set out on beautiful service tables. High back, leather chairs surrounded the conference table. They were very comfortable, which was a good thing because I was in for a long wait.

As I sat in the empty conference room for the next hour or so, I was able to observe that they used an overhead projection system, connected to a PC and a motorized screen. The screen was controlled by a switch on the wall. I know this because I entertained myself by lowering and raising it a couple times while waiting for folks to arrive. This combination of what was cutting-edge technology at the time would be something I would later incorporate into the RB boardroom. But for now, I continued to wait.

It was midmorning on the first day when SBB's CFO, controller, and director of management information joined me in the conference room. We exchanged the usual pleasantries. The CFO then kicked the meeting off by outlining a series of objectives for my visit. His presentation was a list of tasks to be accomplished by the director and myself over the next two and a half days. It quickly became very clear to me that I wasn't there to teach, or to even help, I was there to DO. The controller and the director sat silently as the CFO pontificated for fifteen to twenty minutes. Then he turned the meeting over to the director of management information. Before he and the controller excused themselves, the CFO instructed the director to take me on a tour of the headquarters. With that final task being assigned, they exited both the room and the process. I would not see, nor speak with either the CFO or the controller again.

Left in their place was an older gentleman in his mid-fifties (remember I was only thirty-one at the time), impeccably dressed, and as he spoke, I could clearly tell he was from the northeast. As the door closed behind the controller, the director looked across the table at me, stood up, went over to the coffee, and poured himself a cup. *"Want anything?"* he asked. I responded with a *"No thank you"* and he continued: *"I'm Bob. How was your flight?"* I quipped back a slightly sarcastic response which reflected my level of irritation: *"Better than my morning."* Bob grinned ear to ear and sat back down at the table. Ignoring my comment, he continued: *"Tell me about yourself. I have heard all about your involvement with this project, but tell me about you."* With that, we exchanged verbal resumes and brief family histories. Of course, me being a new father and Bob being a recently new grandfather, we spent time talking about how amazing the little ones were. Bob was from New Jersey, and a couple years earlier, had relocated to take advantage of no income taxes paid within the state of Tennessee. Bob's background, wait for it, was in investment banking (M&A). He had retired from a long and successful career within one of the world's largest banks which was headquartered in New York City. He had taken this job a couple years ago as a way to ease into retirement. He and his wife were settling in to a slower pace of life with less travel, leaving them with more time to enjoy the grandchildren.

"Let's walk around the building, meet some people, and then go get some lunch," Bob proposed. With that, we left the conference room and began what would become a very educational two days. I met most of Bob's team followed by a tour of the boardroom, which was impressive as you can well imagine. From there, we went downstairs and walked through the private banking area, located on the ground floor of the building. This was a particularly well-appointed area of the facility where SBB's high net worth customers came for meetings with their private bankers. The director of SBB's private banking division was a young, dynamic executive. Much like Mrs. K, Janet was a polished, Ivy League-educated professional with high energy, and clearly a force to be reckoned with. Janet, Bob, and I headed to lunch and, wow, did I learn.

These two residents of the SBB subduction zone used concepts, applied financial models, and offered innovative ideas that were light years beyond what RB was currently using. However, over lunch, I was able to offer a new concept that Janet and Bob found interesting. The two SBB leaders were fascinated by RB's objective of pushing the information from the K Corp software into the hands of those at the POS, those most capable of delivering enhanced value to the customer. I was shocked by their reaction to this concept. In my mind, that was the sole purpose behind SBB's interest in my making these trips. Clearly, there had been a huge misunderstanding along the way. Things like this can happen. But a misunderstanding of this size? Doubtful.

No, in this instance, the misunderstanding was an intentional miscommunication, the deliberate withholding of information. This tactic is actually pretty typical within the process of change when it is being managed by the forces of structure, the culture of DO. Remember, the driving force behind SBB's purpose of change, the leader of WHY, was the chairman of the board who was the recently retired CEO. By reputation, the chairman was a brilliant, dynamic, and extremely successful leader. His legacy was one of professionalism, innovation, and vision. Under his leadership, SBB experienced an unprecedented period of growth in both size and shareholder value. So much so that SBB had been nationally recognized many times for their successes. Both Bob and Janet used glowing terms when they spoke of the chairman's past contributions to the SBB culture. However, the terminology they used to describe the current executive leadership was, let's say, more guarded.

Hindsight is always twenty-twenty. Based on experience, here is what I believe happened within SBB. This is typically what happens to innovation when the purpose of change is managed by structure. Mr. K had developed a good relationship with SBB's previous CEO and had maintained that relationship, even after he assumed the role of chairman. When Mr. K and Mr. E developed the foundational concepts around leveraging information at the POS, Mr. K shared the idea with the chairman. SBB's chairman immediately saw the value in the concept behind pushing information out to the POS and began introducing the idea to the new CEO. The CEO, along with his executive team, then skillfully applied objective buffers in combination with the use of external catalysts in an effort to convince the chairman to narrow the scope of the innovation, reducing the risk to SBB and effectively gaining control over the proposal by scaling it down so it would fit into SBB's existing structure. The end result was a change process that was only going to impact Janet's area, private banking. The external catalysts used by SBB had all agreed that delivering enhanced value to the high net worth customers first was a sound strategy. Private banking would be a safe place to test the innovation before rolling it out to the entire SBB organization. The consensus was to test the new concept in Janet's area and then, if proven successful, they could roll the concept out to other parts of the organization. Structure, SBB's culture of DO, was firmly in control.

I will say this again, those who manage change through the use of structure are not bad people and they very rarely hold sinister intent. Just like those who lead change through purpose, their vision of the future may not always be correct, but their intentions are honorable. People are people, regardless of where you find them, and we are all the product of our choices and needs. Let's step back for a moment to gain a wider perspective. SBB had attained a level of success which the executive team wished to protect and preserve. The SBB executive team also saw the storm clouds gathering, but they concluded the best path for the organization was one of risk mitigation through enhanced structure. Their risk-based perspective forced them to view all innovation other than *incremental* improvement as unnecessary risk, especially given the possibility of difficult times ahead. SBB's culture of DO was acting in a manner that they perceived as being in the best interests of their CORE.

I was not in the room during the SBB discussions, but I have been at the table during many similar strategic planning sessions. Based on those experiences, I would imagine the SBB chairman's response was not one of aggressively supporting the opportunity. Rather, I would expect his response was measured, more considered. He most likely listened intently to the presentation of information and to the recommendations of the CEO and his executive team. Much like Mr. E's choice to not fight the battle over RB establishing an ATM network, the chairman decided not to own the change, but rather to support the consensus. At that very moment, structure began to dominate purpose, and long before I was enlisted as a quasi-internal catalyst, the foundation for SBB's change process was set. The culture of DO formed the foundation for change and my role, along with Bob and Janet, was to implement incremental improvement to the private banking process within the established SBB structure.

Do you recall my second one-on-one conversation with Mr. E when I asked him about consensus and he pointed out the difference between the definition of the word consensus and his meaning of the word consensus? Remember when he talked about his becoming "lazy" after RB had attained an acceptable level of success and then he twice said: "My fault"?

Through all my years of helping others to better understand the process of change, I have come to realize that the act of ownership on the part of a change leader is the single most important moment for change. This single action will many times make the difference between the success or failure of WHY in forming the foundation of change. When the individual(s) leading change openly own the result, the purpose of change has become personal, and is now a part of who they are. This process of open ownership is similar in commitment to a leader attaining the fourth human *need*, love, the verb love. Once you own the process of helping others, you are determined to accomplish the mission, regardless of the perceived personal risks. Mr. E chose to own what he viewed as a failure and, therefore, he took ownership of the solution, the purpose, the WHY behind the process of change which was needed to correct the shortfall.

Once you know what to look for, the ability to determine which culture is forming the foundation for change is pretty easy. You can identify the dominate culture by asking, then answering these simple questions: "Are the executive's words being supported by actions? Do their words and deeds match?" For example, all three parties stated how important this process of change was to their respective organizations.

Given what you now know, which two of the three leaders made the effort to communicate? Which two of the three leaders committed significant amounts of personal time and resources to ensure the alignment of purpose with result? Answer: Mr. E and Mr. K. Both Mr. E and Mr. K were leading the process of change and were champions for purpose; therefore, in both organizations, the culture of WHY formed the foundation. Those managing change within SBB chose to commit what little time they allocated to the process in an effort to ensure the alignment of structure with result.

If, at thirty-one years old, I would have known what I knew twenty years later, I would have correctly anticipated SBB's actions. When the CFO and controller finally decided to meet with me in the conference room, they did so after making me wait. This action sent an intentional and clear message: *I was in their world now, and in their world, they ruled.* These actions aligned perfectly with their lack of communication over the prior few months. After all, why should they be talking with me? I didn't understand SBB's internal structure. In their view, I could provide little or no value to SBB until I was told, specifically, what they wanted DOne. The message being sent was further supported by the actions of the CFO who, when he finally made it to the meeting, listed a set of specific tasks for us to accomplish during my short visit to the SBB world.

> *When structure (the culture of DO) forms the foundation, the capacity for change will be restricted, regardless of the size of available resources.*

Whenever the actions of change managers (the individuals working on the front lines and in the trenches) are controlled by proclamations issued from those managing change (the individuals establishing the structure) the culture of DO is in charge. When structure forms the foundation, the capacity for change will be restricted, regardless of the size of available resources.

Whenever the actions of change managers are encouraged by substantive communication and supported through aligned actions from those leading change (the individuals establishing the purpose), the culture of WHY is in charge. When purpose forms the foundation, the capacity for change is limited only by the size of the recourses available to the organization.

> *When purpose (the culture of WHY) forms the foundation, the capacity for change is limited only by the size of the recourses available to the organization.*

I have found these observations to be universally true regardless of the industry, the ownership structure, or the size of the organization. Change managers work on the front lines of change, in the trenches, every working minute of every day. All through the subduction zone, employees and front-line managers are being constantly challenged to turn chaos into some form of efficiency and to forge the problems that pop up into opportunities for enhanced value. The stronger the relationship (trust, integrity, and communication) between the front lines and the dominate culture of change, the more closely the actual results will align with the desired outcome.

> *When structure (DO) forms the foundation for change, the substantive communication to the front lines will be rooted in the new purpose, but will be tightly restricted by established policies, procedures, and time schedules.*

Why is this always true? Answer: when structure forms the foundation for change, the substantive communication to the front lines will be rooted in the new purpose, <u>but</u> will be tightly restricted by established policies, procedures, and time schedules. There will be innovation produced from the efforts of the front lines, but it will result in structured, incremental change. In this environment, risk mitigation is the overriding priority controlling the opportunities for enhanced value, limiting creative capacity.

When purpose forms the foundation for change, the substantive communication to the front lines will be rooted in policies, procedures, and time schedules *and* will be motivated by the new purpose. Innovation produced from the efforts of the front lines will be purposeful, creative change, which may result in massive leaps forward in innovation, limited only by available resources. It is here, only within the environment formed by purpose, where an organization has the chance to reengineer or transform itself.

> *When purpose (WHY) forms the foundation for change, the substantive communication to the front lines will be rooted in policies, procedures, and time schedules and will be motivated by the new purpose.*

So, with all this being said, who was right? Over time, who made the right choices regarding change, leading their respective organization to ultimately succeed? My response to this question is: First, tell me how you define success. And next, give me the time period you are asking about. If we were doing something as simple as playing chess, even multi-dimensional chess, we would know who ultimately won the game. Then we would reset the board and start anew. The process of change is never that simple, never that finite. As we learned earlier, change is a constant companion and our success or failure in leading change is ultimately a function of an individual's perspective.

At the time, serving as a thirty-one-year-old change manager within each of the three processes, my perspective was very different from those held by the leaders and managers of change. From my perspective, which was narrow in scope and formed using a short-term time horizon, SBB's change process was one of missed opportunity. Most likely, those managing the SBB process of change held a different perspective. I would imagine the CEO and his team viewed this process as successful, and as we will discover in a moment, the chairman most likely perceived the SBB process as a success as well. How is it possible for polar opposite perceptions to exist at the same time regarding the same change process? Answer: not only is it possible, but it is the expected norm. To better understand the answer, let's look again at both sides of the coin for our examples.

By the way, not to slight Mr. K in our following examples, but his was a pretty clear outcome. He was completely successful. His definition of success was to *get the coin,* and he certainly accomplished his purpose. His original vision of *the storm clouds on the horizon* created an urgent need for change, which he successfully communicated to RB, SBB, and others. Mr. K took the risks, created the opportunity, and assembled the capacity necessary to innovate and then market his software product. His interest in me was no more than the temporary acquisition of a needed resource, an internal human catalyst, to create needed additional capacity within K Corp's subduction zone. One may read these words and conclude that Mr. K had harmed me in some way, or that he used me to get what he wanted. Of course he used me and my thanks to Mr. K for providing me with the opportunity to learn. The experiences and the perspectives gained through my interactions with Mr. K, Mrs. K, Roger, Ish, and the entire K Corp team became a part of who I was and who I would become. But, what was the learning opportunity within SBB? We will return to finish the story portion of *Tennessee in July* in a moment, but first I need to make one more important point.

One of the many life lessons I would learn from my brief time at SBB was, in this instance, SBB's chairman chose to yield to the forces of structure. By yielding purpose to the culture of DO, SBB limited the potential innovation from this particular change process. Was the chairman right in doing so? Let's see. Recall the three rules of leadership. **Leadership Rule #1: Always be professional,**

> ## The three rules
> ## of leadership

which begins with respect for yourself and everyone around you. As the chairman, he respected the opinions and recommendations of the CEO and his team; therefore, he was correct. **Leadership Rule #2: Always strive to work smarter, not harder.** Janet's division, SBB's private banking group, did work smarter after the changes were implemented so, yes, SBB was successful. **Leadership Rule #3: Maintain balance in life, have fun!** Now we are getting to the heart of the matter. Maintaining balance in life, the ability to actually enjoy the process of change (having fun in your work), becomes a major challenge for most leaders. To actually look forward to leading change, one must first understand the process of change. Then, once change is understood, the successful leader will strive to experience additional change processes, learning from each new encounter. The more they learn, and the more they understand, the more skilled at leading change the individual will become. Because the process of change is a constant companion, the learning experiences accumulate quickly.

For several years, the SBB chairman had been successfully leading change, willing the culture of WHY to be the foundational force for change within his organization. Rule #3 requires a leader to maintain balance, personally and professionally. As I mentioned earlier, neither DO nor WHY can exist in their pure forms over an extended period of time. They depend on each other to balance out growth. Too much structure, over too long of a period, squashes innovation through ever-increasing restriction. Too much purpose, without structure, squashes innovation through resulting chaos. During his tenure as CEO, the chairman had successfully challenged the SBB culture to innovate, seeking ever greater purpose through each new change process. From the chairman's perspective, the change process involving K Corp's software offered a good opportunity to inject additional structure into the SBB culture, serving to better organize existing purpose and reducing organizational risk. It was, indeed, a good time for him to re-balance the cultures in order to enhance the long-term value of the franchise.

Again, with the use of twenty-twenty hindsight, given SBB's cultural needs, coupled with their considerable financial strength and available resources, the chairman was correct in his choice to step back, accept the consensus, and allow the forces of structure to implement this particular change process. My perception was short term. I saw only the single, missed opportunity. His perception was one borne of a long-term, much broader perspective. To bolster that point, we need only roll the clock forward a few years. SBB would eventually be acquired by Southern Mega Bank for what was an eye-opening amount of stock and cash. The long-term perspective the chairman held regarding the process of change successfully served the needs of his Core of Responsibility (CORE). FYI: the CORE is a reference to the three core groups leadership must serve when implementing cultural transformation. The three core groups are the customers, shareholders, and culture of the organization (see the related sections in Books One and Two).

Recall when we stated that most see the constant, ever-present process of change as either an ally or an enemy? Then we added that the successful leader learns to view change as a companion. This is a good place to point out that we all have a second, ever-present companion, which is *time*. As with change, time is usually viewed by individuals as either an ally or an enemy when it too should be viewed as a second lifelong companion. The processes of change and time are inseparable. If we continue with our analogy of playing a game of chess, the processes of change and time form the red and black squares on the board, regardless of the board's size. The three rules of leadership apply equally to both processes. To successfully lead the processes of change and time, the three rules of leadership must always be respected, worked with intelligently, and kept in balance.

At this point, you may be asking yourself: "Where is the third element? Rob always works in threes. Three leadership rules. Three sides to the triangles that are used to form each model. We have change and time. What is the missing, third companion?" An excellent observation and you would be correct. There is a third constant companion for all leaders. When viewing the model for teaching the intangible concepts involving success, this third piece would form the foundation of the equilateral triangle. The answer to your question is: *perspective.* Perspective is our third, ever-present companion.

Let's go back to the concepts around *two sides of the same coin.* Change, time, and perspective all work together each time we go to assess our successes or failures. SBB's and RB's leaders, in fact all leaders, base their judgments, their choices, on knowledge guided by experience. The filter through which knowledge and experiences are viewed is shaped by perspective. Each leader, in fact every individual, has their own unique set of perspectives, filters, through which they process information and view results.

RB's and SBB's leaders of change saw the exact same set of future challenges facing their respective organizations, the storm clouds gathering on the horizon. Both were presented with the same solution, K Corp's software. The two held the same expectations for success, created by the leveraging of information at the POS in order to enhance value. Each leader was focused on serving the needs of their CORE. How can all of these factors be the same, and the process of change be implemented differently and yet, both leaders be correct in their choices? Answer: they both followed all three leadership rules, including Rule #3: maintain balance.

SBB was coming off of a protracted period of time where purpose had constantly formed the foundation of change. In order to reestablish balance, SBB needed more structure. Within RB, the culture was caught in the throes of a protracted period where structure formed the foundation for change, as demonstrated by the consensus presented in opposition to establishing the ATM network. When Mr. E stated "my fault," he took ownership of the re-balancing process. Mr. E realized the need for the culture to return to a perspective similar to when he first came to RB. Mr. E needed to reestablish balance by injecting more purpose into RB's change process. To reestablish balance within RB, he needed to lead the process of change so that purpose formed its foundation, freeing up innovation and driving the organization to greater levels of success. He knew that there would be the right time for structure to once again become the foundation for change, but not today.

On the other side of the coin, within SBB, it was time for structure to take the lead. Both leaders were proven correct in their choices. Both leaders effectively led change to successfully meet the needs of their respective COREs. And, of course, Mr. K placed the coin in his corporate pocket. And why not? He earned it.

That's enough time spent, for now, delving into our lifelong companions of change, time, and perspective. You can be sure that we will revisit them within the last chapter when we put the concepts together in order to construct the *Capacity for Understanding* model. But, for now, I still had some learning to do, so let's get back to my lunch meeting with Bob and Janet.

This was my first day on-site at SBB's headquarters in Tennessee. After a morning of *hurry up and wait,* I received a list of tasks to be accomplished, which were delivered to me by the CFO during a thirty-minute meeting. Joining me on this journey was SBB's director of management information, Bob, a skilled and experienced financial analyst. Bob had joined SBB a couple years earlier after a successful career in investment banking (M&A) within one of the nation's largest money center banks, headquartered in New York. After we spent a few minutes getting to know a little more about each other's background, Bob took me on a tour of SBB's impressive headquarters. We ended our tour in the private banking area where we met Janet, the area's director. The three of us headed to a working lunch where I discovered: (1) that SBB was light-years ahead of RB in their application of technology and their level of understanding regarding the business of banking; and (2) they had no idea that RB's process involved pushing the new technology out to all POS locations. SBB's change process had been restricted to a much narrower scope than RB's process, impacting Janet's area only.

Clearly, Bob, Janet, and I were members of SBB's change management team. The three of us, and several other SBB employees, were working in the trenches of the subduction zone created by the Plate Tectonics of Change. It was also unmistakable that the culture of DO, structure, had formed the foundation for this particular change process. If I had only known then what I know now regarding the cultures of change, I could have helped Bob and Janet establish a set of more realistic expectations. But, at that time, I didn't understand the forces at work, so the three of us dug in and started to make change happen (just as those working in the trenches always do). Bob arranged for me to spend the rest of the afternoon with a couple of his top system programmers. Janet returned to her area and started to gather for my review that evening as much publicly available information about SBB's history, financial performance, and product/service brochures as she could find. The information from Janet was critical for me if I was going to be able to effectively help Bob's programmers.

The more I knew about SBB and their products, the better guide I could become. My value as the internal human catalyst was to serve as a guide, directing Bob's programmers to the correct area of the software where the data they needed was stored. The programmers would then design an extract that would strip the needed data from K Corp's software and create what they termed a *flat file*. This extracted file could then be exported to a PC and manipulated by one of Bob's financial analysts. Please forgive my use of archaic terminology (I hope I used the correct terms), but it is important to remember that all of this was taking place during a time when mainframe–based computing ruled the world and PCs were still a curiosity. Bottom line, we created a series of interface tables which were mapped to specific cells within K Corp's system. By midafternoon of the second day, we had a conference room filled with empty coffee cups and pizza boxes. We also had about a dozen flip chart sheets taped to the wall which contained the map for locating the information Bob wanted and Janet needed. Part one of my mission had been accomplished. SBB had secured what they wanted out of this exchange.

The second part of my mission was to learn whatever I could regarding SBB's M&A process. Given the confidential nature of M&A, I knew going in that there would be tight restrictions on what information SBB could share. However, during our meeting with the CFO and controller, one of the tasks assigned was for Bob to arrange a meeting between myself and SBB's lead M&A executive, Tom. I had high hopes that this meeting would provide me with insight as to what made their M&A process so successful. Bob had arranged the meeting for the morning of the second day. Tom canceled the meeting at the last minute and rescheduled it for that afternoon. As the afternoon wore on, that meeting was also canceled. Around noon on the third day, I needed to head to the airport and catch my flight home. We were running out of time for rescheduling the meeting. Bob apologized to me for the delay, but promised that the meeting would take place as scheduled the next morning. As is often the case, when one door closes on an opportunity, another door will open and so it was with this meeting.

Bob felt badly that I had delivered on my side of the bargain, but to this point, SBB had not delivered on their part of the agreement. Given the meeting for that afternoon had been canceled and the programmers had what they needed, Bob offered me a choice. He suggested that I could return to my hotel room early and enjoy some well-deserved down time, or we could go to his office where he would show me how he intended to use the information we had mapped. Another chance to learn, let's go!

Over the next few hours, one question led to two more and the education I received on data mining was invaluable. Bob knew financial ratios that I had never heard of. Not only did he know how to calculate them, he also knew how to apply them, and most importantly, he knew why they were important. He taught me how to apply ratio analysis in order to assess the current market value of an organization. Then, he took the same models, and showed me how to project future performance when given a series of assumed variables. Basically, Bob showed me how to build a set of pre-merger, proforma financial statements and to roll them forward into a set of statements for the resulting combined company, post-merger.

We continued our discussions over dinner that evening. At the end of the second day, by the time I made it back to my hotel room, I felt like my head was going to explode from all that I had learned. It would take me months of working on my own, along with countless trials and errors, before I would finally construct my first RB-based model for franchise valuation. RB had more than gotten its money's worth and I still had the meeting in the morning with SBB's lead M&A guy. That was going to be *something*... it was *something* all right.

The first part of the next morning was spent with Bob's program-mers, reviewing output and making final corrections to the map. At around 10:00 that morning, Bob came in to get me and we walked down the hall to the corporate boardroom. As we were walking down the hall, Bob assured me that the meeting was really going to happen this time because he had seen Tom in the CFO's office just a couple minutes ago. At 10:10, Tom's ego arrived. At 10:15, Tom himself made it to the boardroom. I shouldn't say that, but it was true. Tom was bigger than life. He was one of the most self-confident individuals I had ever met. In sales terminology, Tom was a legitimate *rainmaker* (the ability to consistently generate success where others fail). This guy could bring the rain in the middle of the desert during a drought, and he wanted everybody to know it. The moment he hit the door, he started talking: *"So they tell me you want to learn about M&A. I have fifteen minutes before I have to leave for the country club. Do you play golf?"* I assumed he was talking to me, so I answered: *"No sir."* Tom shot back: *"Then learn! More business is done on the links than anywhere else."* By this time, Tom was leaning up against the service table, directly across from where I was sitting, and was tossing back some grapes. Pointing at Bob, he continued: *"Bean counters, like Bob, think that buying companies is all about making the numbers work. Those Wall Street types have never closed a deal in their lives.*" I glanced at Bob and he had a sheepish grin fixed on his face and he kept it there the entire time Tom was talking. Tom continued: "*It is all about the social issues! Numbers are for the bean count-ers. The real decisions are always made around the social issues. Who runs the surviving company? Who goes onto the board and how many seats do they get? Who keeps their job? Who has to move to what city? Social issues. You can't solve those on one of Bob's spreadsheets. Don't get me wrong, Bob and his guys are important. Right, Bob? Love ya. But, almost all the deals that fall apart do so after everybody has agreed on the price. Social issues! Those get solved on the golf course, at the ballpark, or over dinner. Face to face. You ever sold anything or are you just a numbers guy?*" Again, I assumed he was talking to me, so I responded: "*Yes. I made a very good living over four or five years selling copiers on straight commission. I understand the importance of finding the real decision maker. Face to face is the only way.*" Tom seemed to be shocked by my answer. Bob didn't react at all. He was just sitting there with the same silly smile plastered on his face. Tom replied: "*There may be hope for you, after all. I've got to go. Bob, we need to talk about a new deal. I will call you later today.*" Tom glided out of the room with his ego firmly in tow.

We both sat there silent for a moment. Bob was still smiling, then he broke the silence: "*He's from the west coast! I should have warned you, but how would you prepare someone for Tom?*" Bob got up from his chair and turned in my direction: "*Listen to him. Take what he says about the social issues to heart because he is right. I can't tell you the hours I have spent hammering out the last financial details, only to have the deal blown out of the water because some CEO wants another seat on the board or doesn't like the town where the new headquarters will be located. Successful M&A is more of an art than a science.*

"*Well, that pretty much wraps us up. You've got to get to the airport and I've got to figure out what Tom is up to. I can't thank you enough for all your help. Have a safe flight.*" And with that being said, we shook hands and parted ways. Bob and I did speak briefly over the phone a couple times in the next few weeks, but I never did make that second trip to Tennessee. It wasn't needed. We had put into place enough structure for SBB's change process to go forward. Mission accomplished. Time to head home.

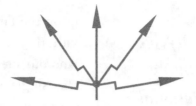

Epilog for Life Lesson I and Introduction to Life Lesson II

Change. Time. Perspective. These three lifelong companions are influenced each day by human *needs* and *choices*. Together, these five elements form our individual *capacity for understanding*. In turn, our capacity for understanding forms the foundation for all transformation and growth, both as an individual and as a leader. If I had chosen to be less curious, or perceived the purpose of my visit to SBB as a waste of time, I would have closed the door on a giant opportunity to learn. As time passed, and my responsibilities within RB changed, the knowledge I gained from this one trip to Tennessee became an important part of the foundation I used for my later responsibilities in M&A, cultural transformation, and leading change. Sure, these events taken by themselves did not provide a direct path to success, but growth is always the result of an accumulation of experiences. Growth is an accumulation of change, over time, viewed through the prism of different perspectives.

Tolerance. The willingness to understand. The courage to continue moving forward in spite of the risks. The strength of purpose to remain focused when facing distraction. These are the characteristics needed to realize the benefits offered by tolerance. The capacity for understanding, the foundational requirement for all learning and growth, fuels our individual ability for tolerance. Think back on the entire series of events I relayed within Life Lesson I. The accumulation of my experiences from GRC, previous employers, and growing

> *The capacity for understanding, the foundational requirement for all learning and growth, fuels our individual ability for tolerance.*

up on the farm all provided me with the capacity to raise my hand during the ATM meeting. That single act put into motion a series of events which led to an additional set of opportunities, accumulating even more experiences, each time increasing my capacity for understanding. At any point during this sequence of events, I could have *chosen* to be less curious or perceived a *need* for more security. What if I never raised my hand? What if, after my meeting with RB's CFO, Mr. E had not sent a message which refocused me on the future? What if Roger didn't perceive me as the *real deal*? What if I chose not to attend the conference in April? What if I was discouraged after my first on-site meeting at SBB or became distracted by Tom's flamboyant demeanor? What if…?

Each of us progress along the Cycle of Human Development (Books One and Two) through a series of experiences. Each experience expands or contracts the Universe of Present Facts available to us. It is from this universe we extract the data which will form the additional/ new information we will use to help shape our perspective. The *perspective* we hold regarding the *changes* we encounter over the course of *time* is constantly evolving to reflect our *choices* and to meet our *needs*. The resulting *capacity for understanding* establishes our level of tolerance for future change or diversity of perspective.

Interesting concept, isn't it? We will drill down a little further into the concept of *capacity for understanding* in the last section of this book. Let's label the increased capacity for understanding as *maturity*. The accepted norm is that maturity is a function of accumulated experiences over time. Actually, it is much, much more than the linear passage of time. But, for now, we'll allow that definition to stand.

Over the next twenty years, I continued to accumulate experiences as a leader and as an individual. I would spend the next nine years or so working and growing within the RB organization. There were so many life lessons during this period, so many opportunities for me to learn. Actually, the story which forms the foundation for Book Two is based on just one of those experiences within RB. In December of 2000, I moved on from RB to gain more experience by serving in a leadership position within a small, local Federal Savings Bank (LFSB).

Leading within LFSB was one of the best, most rewarding experiences of my professional life (so far). What made it different? From day one, when I walked through the doors of LFSB, I had a clear understanding of our strategic short-term and longer-term purposes. My short-term purpose was to find what needs fixed and figure a way to fix it. Basically, I was to lead change, manage change, and serve as the primary change manager. The leadership role I assumed was dependent on where we were in the process.

The long-term objective was to cause a sustainable increase in LFSB's franchise value, and once that was accomplished, it was to find the most effective way to transfer that value to its CORE (customers, shareholders, and culture). Over the course of the next five years, both the short-term and the long-term strategic purposes were accomplished. As is always the case, the reason for our success was tied directly to the individuals which made up the LFSB team. Great people, following a consistent purpose, working within a balanced change process. During most of this five-year period, the foundation for change was solidly rooted in the culture of WHY. However, when needed, structure would lead the way in order to maintain balance, reducing the chaos of WHY and allowing us to enjoy the process.

One of my personal rules is to never look back. Once I leave an organization, I will have very little contact with those I left behind. Why? It is out of respect for the organization's leadership. LFSB is the single exception to this rule. It has been over fourteen years since I left LFSB, but I still visit with several of the leaders from that organization on a regular basis. They are good, personal friends and will always have my respect.

My purpose being completed, I parted from LFSB in the first half of 2005. At the age of forty-seven, I went to the house with the intention to stay there. I told everyone that I was going to "retire." After all, I had been in a suit and tie every workday since I was nineteen. I had spent the prior twenty-eight years in leadership, leading people, change, and organizations. When I left LFSB, I viewed change as my ally and time was an enemy to be defeated at every turn. I needed to reestablish balance in my life. I *needed* a break and, by this point, we had been blessed with enough financial success that we could afford for me to take advantage of some down time.

Over the first three months of my "retirement," I kept a list of tasks and attacked it each day. Change was still an ally and time still needed to be defeated. After about ninety days of working like a mad man on projects, I began to ease off a little. Driving our son to and from school became something I looked forward to each day. I found myself no longer switching into full boss mode when I heard the phone ring. If I finished my list of tasks for the day, fine. If I didn't get everything on the list done, that was fine too. And yes, I kept a list and I still do today because it makes me feel better, it keeps me organized, and it keeps me focused. Bottom line, I was regaining my balance. Life was beginning to become fun and for the next few months, especially through the holiday season, I was as happy as I had ever been. As the winter months wore on, I found myself reflecting on the accumulated experiences from the prior twenty-eight years. What worked and what didn't? Most importantly, I spent time attempting to understand the "why" behind previous successes and failures. It was during this time, the first quarter of 2006, when I began to assemble the notes for what would eventually become the *LIVE better LEAD differently* series of books.

As the spring of 2006 rolled around, I was beginning to think about what was next. Where do I go from here? Everybody, but me, knew that I could never stay on the sidelines for long. So, it was no surprise to anyone when I started talking about finding something new to get into. It was March or April of 2006 when the phone rang. One of my friends from LFSB served on the board of directors for the regional medical system (RMS), a not-for-profit organization. This was the area's largest employer, by far, and served as the economic engine for our entire region. RMS had the need for a person to find what needed to be fixed and figure a way to fix it. This was the exact same short-term purpose I had served when working at LFSB. My friend had no doubt that I could help the organization and was reaching out to see if I was interested in getting back to work.

I knew RMS's CEO and the majority of the RMS board of directors through networking, serving on a foundation board, and my work within various community organizations, but I was unfamiliar with RMS's executive leadership team. After discussing the options with Jennifer, I decided to interview for the position. It was here, during the interview process, where the similarities between this opportunity and my experiences from the RB story contained in Life Lesson I began to align. As you read Life Lesson II, you will discover that many of the circumstances I encountered were eerily similar, even though they took place in a completely different industry (health care vs. financial services) within a totally different ownership structure (community based, not-for-profit vs. publicly traded, shareholder owned, and very much for profit). I would venture to say that you will be shocked as to the similarities. Be assured as you read Life Lesson II and tell yourself that this couldn't have really happened this way, that I am relaying what actually happened.

Please keep in mind that I have found the principles and rules established in this book and the prior two books to be universal. No matter what industry, regardless of the organizational structure, people will always be people, and as individuals, they will always reflect their *choices* and *needs*. Individuals all learn through the application of the Cycle of Human Development. Change, time, perspective, and the capacity for understanding are with us all as we progress through life.

It is how we each apply these elements that creates the diversity among us. What I find fascinating is, once you know what to look for, you will be amazed at how many times you will encounter the same patterns of behavior. Once you learn to see the first set of patterns, you will begin to see these common signs everywhere, and they will serve to guide you on your journey. That is the wonder of growth and why we should never stop learning.

> *Change, time, perspective, and the capacity for understanding are with us all as we progress through life. It is how we each apply these elements that creates the diversity among us.*

When I walked into my first interview, which was with RMS's CFO, I had no idea what to expect. I had never met the gentleman. After being kept waiting in the lobby for several minutes, I was escorted back to a conference room. The room was first class. High back leather chairs surrounded a beautifully constructed conference table. I sat down in one of the comfortable chairs and waited, and waited. Another thirty minutes passed. Is this beginning to sound familiar? Just wait, it gets better.

When the CFO finally arrived, he apologized for the delay and dove right into the interview by listing a series of requirements and expectations for the job. He then told me: *"I see you have no background in health care. Health care is very complex, way more complicated than banking. You really need to think about whether or not you want to take on such a challenge. Health care is not for everybody. I want you to take some time and think about what you are about to get into. I just left the CEO's office and he tells me that you are the person we want for this job. I told him that I have my doubts. For this level of position, the medical center always attempts to recruit someone with at least an advanced degree or certification, usually an MBA, CPA or both. You will be on a very steep learning curve. Think about it and let me know if you want to come back to talk about the position. Why don't you call me on Monday next week and let me know what you have decided? It was nice meeting you, Rob. Let me walk you out."*

Look at all the signs! Based on what you already know, between the CEO and the CFO, who is attempting to lead change (purpose) and who is managing change (structure)? Although he was more subtle than RB's CFO, RMS's CFO's use of fear and intimidation in order to manipulate my decision was identical. Did you spot his mistake? What was the statement he made that kept me coming back for more? Answer: his mistake was when he told me what the CEO had said: *"…. that you are the person we want for this job."* From the very beginning, this first interview was a proclamation of expectations in an attempt to establish control over my future actions. The forces of DO were definitely on the move. Making me wait, the ornate furnishings in the room, posture, attitude, tone of voice, etc. were exactly what I had seen before. What do you think? Did I keep constant eye contact with the CFO during this first meeting?

I had just spent the last nine months establishing balance, reflecting on what I had learned over the prior twenty-eight years. The CFO had no way of knowing it, but he had just thrown down a challenge from which I couldn't walk away. If I truly believed in what I had been learning and teaching, this was the perfect opportunity for me to apply my skills. On Monday, I called the CFO and expressed my interest in continuing the interview process. His calendar was full that week, but the following week, he had time to meet with me (more waiting). The appointment was set and kept.

To make a long story short, the second interview was more of the same from the CFO. The difference was that this time, the CEO, Ted, wanted to interview me. Usually, when an additional person enters an interview, the person conducting the interview stays in the room. Not in this case. As soon as the CEO entered the conference room, the CFO got up and left. Curious? As I mentioned earlier, I knew Ted from various community functions, and I knew most of RMS's board.

We exchanged pleasantries, then got down to business. Ted leaned back in the chair, put his feet up on the conference table, and said: *"Rob, the job is yours if you want it and RMS is lucky to get you. This is not going to be easy. You can already see that we have work to do and you will be pretty much on your own for a while. We can't pay you anything close to what you are used to earning."* Ted paused and then completed his thought: *"RMS has grown a lot over the last ten years and we are going to continue growing. When you grow at this rate, there are always areas that get left behind or places where you can do things better. That is what I need you to focus on. I understand you are a 'fixer.' We need a fixer. You in?"* I replied: *"Ted, this is our home. RMS is the main economic driver in our area. If you think I can help, I'm in."* Ted responded: *"Great. I'll let HR know to expect you next Monday morning. We have an orientation class starting that morning and we will get you in it. Welcome to RMS, Rob."* With that being said, he stood up, shook my hand, and escorted me out the door.

On Monday morning, I began orientation with about thirty other new hires, mostly clinical professionals. Orientation lasted through Tuesday afternoon, at which time our direct supervisor was to pick us up from the class and take us on a tour of our new area, introducing us to our new team members. During orientation, I discovered that my direct supervisor was the CFO. I sat in the room after orientation was completed, and as the group dwindled, the CFO was nowhere to be seen. After everyone was gone, the instructor said she would make a call and see who was supposed to meet me. A few minutes later, the CEO's administrative assistant (admin) came through the door, apologized for the confusion, and escorted me to the parking lot. It was here that I learned that I was a department of one. I had no direct reports, no support staff, and no office yet. Ted's admin told me to go on home and tomorrow report to the accounting area which was located about five miles off RMS's main campus. Armed with the address I needed for my trip in the morning, I headed home.

Around 7:30 the next morning, I was in the parking lot at the address I had been given. Those who have read Book One will appreciate this irony. My new office was going to be located inside a building which, at one time, was a retail store for the discount chain where I had my first leadership experiences. Years after I had moved on, the company had been sold and the new owners eventually took the chain into bankruptcy, selling all of its store locations. RMS had purchased this particular site to serve as temporary office space, its warehouse, and a retail location for medical equipment.

As with all RMS locations, the building required the scanning of your ID in order to gain access. My ID would not work which was no surprise being it was my first day at this location, so I waited for someone else to arrive. After a short wait, another team member came up to the door. I asked if they could let me inside. The answer was no, but they would check with the controller to see if I could come in. A few minutes later, I was standing in the hall outside of the controller's office waiting in line for my turn to see him. Eventually we met and he showed me to my 'office.' *"Sorry,"* he said as he pointed to what was to be my new office. *"We just found out yesterday afternoon that you were coming. I will let IT know you are here."* And with that, he returned to his office to answer his constantly ringing phone.

My new office was a windowless storage room, about the size of a large closet. Inside the area was a small desk, a broken chair, a disconnected phone, and a monitor (with no computer). Against the walls on both sides of the desk, boxes were stacked from the floor to a height above my head. There were no office supplies of any type. I thanked the controller and carefully sat down on the broken chair. I had brought my own paper and a pen just in case. I pulled them out, laid them on the empty desk, and smiled. I was getting the idea that, just maybe, I was not really welcome at RMS. First things first, I found the coffee and the restroom. Okay, that's a start. After finishing my coffee, I had concluded that no one was going to take me around and introduce me to the other employees in the building. And, certainly, no one was going to call me on my disconnected phone, e-mail me on my non-existent computer to see how I was doing, or issue a list of tasks for the day.

At this point, it would have been very easy for me to tell RMS: "Thank you, but no thank you." The message I was receiving was, on the surface, loud and clear: "Go home! We don't need you and we don't want your kind messing up our existing structure." What kept me from dropping off my new badge at HR and heading to the house? Answer: experience and the ability to view the circumstances from a different perspective. Think back. I had seen all of this before. This is the same tune as I encountered at RB and SBB, just a different dance. The culture of DO ruled RMS with an iron fist. The words I had heard during orientation were all about purpose, a very well-defined purpose, but every action I had witnessed, up to this point, was clearly controlled by structure. I was already there, so why not take some time and explore my surroundings? It was time for me to go out and meet some of the good folks working in the trenches. After all, I had nothing else to do.

Know what I found when I spoke with the team members in the trenches? Wonderful people, working hard every day in order to support those who were helping our patients to heal. Each day that passed, I was more and more convinced of the opportunities buried within RMS. The capacity for growth was easy to see, but it was just so tightly restricted by structure that, everywhere I went, I found high levels of stress, frustration, and fear. Other than during the orientation class, there was virtually no communication regarding purpose. There was, however, no end of structure provided through the latest policy or procedure, which was enforced by a clearly defined list of punishments associated with the violation of either.

Turns out, within the building where my new "office" was located, I was surrounded by those working in the trenches. Just down the hallways outside my door, I had access to: accounting; payroll; internal audit; purchasing; inventory management; accounts payable; couriers; and facilities maintenance. Where my office was located was viewed by those in control as a form of punishment, being banished to a windowless closet in an off-campus location. In fact, I saw this as a great place to be. I happened to land right in the heart of the "backroom" trenches. It took about four weeks for my phone to be hooked up and for me to get a computer. During this time, I got to know most of the non-exec support team members. By the end of the first week, I had a chair that was safe to sit in, courtesy of my new friends in facilities maintenance. Purchasing let me borrow a flip chart, some markers, and some tape. I purchased my own office supplies. Inventory management (the warehouse guys) had moved all of the boxes out of my office and had located a filing cabinet for me to use. I had acquired stacks of internal financial reports and public filings which had been provided by internal audit and accounting. I had been on guided tours of our information technology areas, our marketing department, and our billing departments.

By the end of the second week when the CFO came to see me for two minutes, after concluding his meeting just down the hall with the controller, I had acquired a working knowledge of RMS's support processes and historical financial results. The CFO asked me how I was getting along, to which I responded: *"Just fine. Can you help me get a phone and computer? Both would be helpful."* After expressing the appropriate levels of shock and surprise that I was still not connected to the outside world, he assured me that he would see to it immediately. Then, the CFO turned around and left the building.

By now, you may be thinking that I was being pretty slow on the uptake. Clearly, these folks didn't want me around, so why didn't I take the hint? Answer: again, it is all about perspective. As I listened and learned from those working in the trenches, I discovered that my circumstances were, unfortunately, not that unusual within RMS. This was a company expanding so fast that it was common for new team members to show up for work and no one in their department knew they had been hired. The fact that I had a place to sit was almost a luxury. And, as for the delay in getting a phone and a computer, it turned out that the network hub which served our building had been maxed out months ago and no one would take the risk of approving the request to purchase a larger hub without first getting the CFO's authorization. I discovered that, due to my title as a department director, RMS policy gave me the authority to authorize the purchase of the needed equipment. The purchasing department put together the required paperwork and I signed it. By the middle of my fourth week of employment, I had a working phone and my computer was connected, all thanks to the director of purchasing.

During my first month at RMS, I had gained an understanding of the basic risks, untapped capacity, and opportunities within the organization. My understandings were based on my perceptions so, over time, my understandings would be tested through actual experience. I had also established the beginning of several productive relationships with those working and leading in the trenches. There are so many stories that come to mind from my first couple of years working and learning within RMS, but two stories are critical for me to pass on. The first story took place about four months into my tenure with RMS. This story was actually used as the introduction to Book One, *LIVE better LEAD differently, A Transitional Conversation*. The second critical story forms the basis for this book's next section, Life Lesson II. The events I am about to share took place two years after I had joined the medical center.

Just for the purpose of context, RMS was an independent, not-for-profit organization servicing an area roughly the size of the state of New Jersey, with a couple dozen outreach locations and a main hospital with 485 acute care beds. It was the region's largest employer, with approximately four thousand employees, making it the primary economic engine within a struggling, local economy. I had been a department of one, the director of financial operations, which lasted for less than six months. In addition to my financial operations duties, about four months into my RMS tenure, I had taken on the leadership role for the hospital's billing department, which quickly grew to include the hospital's scheduling, registration, and medical records departments. At this point, somewhere during my second year at RMS, I had two offices. One office was located in the administration building directly across the hall from the CFO's office. My second office was a corner office in the hospital billing department located in a building we leased only a few hundred yards off of RMS's main campus. And, by the way, both offices had windows as well as phones and computers that actually worked. Hot dog, life was good!

Relaying all of these circumstances helps to set the scene for *Life Lesson II – Change from the perspective of a fifty-year-old leader.* As I wrote Life Lesson II, I intentionally stayed away from summarizing the life lessons being learned. This is your journey to explore. What can you glean from the circumstances being described? Which of the two cultures are foundational? At what point does the shift to the culture of WHY occur and will it successfully form the foundation for the process of change going forward? And, most importantly, what perspective must I and others maintain in order to increase our capacity for understanding?

All of these questions and many more will pop into your mind as you work your way through Life Lesson II. There is one other observation that will jump out at you from the very beginning. The experiences from Life Lesson I and the experiences from Life Lesson II have many similarities even though they took place in completely different industries and twenty years apart. Those common guideposts which you will discover are real, actual occurrences. The takeaway for you is this: change is a constant, and as a constant, the process of change will display many of the same characteristics within a culture. Always remember that *people are people* no matter where you find them. And, because they all have the same basic human *needs* and make the same *choices*, they exhibit certain characteristics regardless of the cultural setting. Whether you are dealing with people in the boardroom or at the kitchen table, the bottom line is, you are dealing with people. The goal is for you to learn to read the signs that individuals will offer along the way and to gain the capacity for understanding what the signs are telling you.

After we complete this part of our journey together, I will summarize what I believe to be the most valuable takeaways from this experience. As you read, please keep in mind that this is just one thin slice of the whole experience. Also, this is my journey and it will pale when compared to the meaning held within your own experiences. The object is for you to read about how I learned and use my examples as reference points to help you reflect on your own experiences. Once again, it is the benefit gained from each experience which reinforces the fact that we should never stop learning! And now, *Life Lesson II - Change from the perspective of a fifty-year-old leader.*

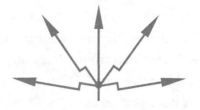

Life Lesson II
CHANGE FROM THE PERSPECTIVE OF A FIFTY-YEAR-OLD LEADER

Closed Doors, Open Opportunities

"Hey Rob, you got a minute?" were the words shouted from the CFO's office directly across the hall from my office in RMS's administration building. Dan had been CFO at RMS for several years. The same could be said for most if not all of RMS's senior leadership team. The members of RMS's senior group were, to the person, extremely intelligent, well-educated, and very high energy. They also shared several other common traits. All of them had been recruited or promoted and taught by Ted, the CEO. Ted was a gifted health care administrator and had served as CEO of RMS for an unusually long time, ten or twelve years. The vast majority of this leadership team had been in health care their entire careers. As a group, they had turned around a struggling, much smaller hospital and grown it into the regional powerhouse. When it came to economic impact, health care innovation, community leadership, etc., RMS was the market's eight-hundred-pound gorilla. With almost a million square feet of newly constructed or recently renovated buildings on the main campus, RMS was an impressive site to behold.

I had been with RMS for about two years at this point. When I heard Dan's invitation to meet, I knew what the topic would be. *"Yes sir,"* I responded and hopped up from behind my desk to head across the hall. As I entered his office, the CFO made a hand gesture that let me know to close the door behind me. Once I sat down in front of his desk, Dan launched into the heart of the matter: *"We have our meeting with Ted in about thirty minutes. This will be your first meeting with him as one of the new vice presidents* (there were a total of four new VPs who had been recently promoted). *The **senior group** has already discussed the content of this meeting with Ted. He always talks with the **senior group** when it is important. During this meeting, Ted is going to show us a video about the dangers of groupthink. Then he is going to ask us what we think about the message from the video. When he asks for your opinion, he really doesn't want to hear what you think. All that Ted is looking for is consensus within the leadership team. One of **us** (a member of the senior group) will respond to Ted and that will set the tone for the rest of the meeting. You're pretty good at reading people, so you do what you think is best during the meeting, but this being your first meeting as a VP, I would recommend saying as little as possible."*

Dan's phone rang and he swiveled his chair around to see who was calling. It was Ted's admin, Debbie, so Dan immediately answered the call. After he hung up, Dan continued: *"That was Debbie. Ted wants to meet with his **senior team** in his office before the meeting with the entire group starts. The start of your meeting will probably be delayed while **we** meet with Ted. Go on over to the boardroom and wait with the others. We'll be there as soon as **we** are finished."* *"Sounds good,"* I replied. I walked across the hall, put on my suit jacket, and headed across the street to the boardroom.

The boardroom was a very nice conference room, located on the ground floor of the main hospital. It was situated directly across the street from the City Park. One side of the room was mostly glass and afforded beautiful views year-round. The main entrance to the boardroom was a set of large, wooden double doors which opened into RMS's dining area. RMS's café was a large area which served patients, guests, and the community at large. The café had its own chef. He and his staff frequently catered meetings and events within the medical center. This meeting was to be a working lunch catered by the café. I was looking forward to a good meal.

As I entered the café, I noticed the double doors to the boardroom were still closed. I was a few minutes early, so I sat down at one of the tables and waited for the room to open up. In a couple minutes, I was joined at the table by Hank, one of the new VPs. Hank was in charge of buildings, the grounds, all construction, food services, maintenance, etc. and etc. I had gotten to know this guy pretty well during my couple of years at RMS. Hank was great. A few years my senior, Hank had been at the medical center for most of his working life. If you wanted to know about RMS's history, talk to Hank. If you wanted to know the latest, talk to Hank. This guy was connected to the community as well as anything going on at RMS. When the doors opened, out walked several of RMS's board members. Hank and I knew all of these guys, so they joined us at the table and we visited on various topics until it was time for our meeting to start. Actually, the CFO had to come and get Hank and me because everyone had already been seated for the meeting and we were still out in the café talking with the directors.

When I walked into the room, the conference table had been transformed into an ornate banquet table with china and all the appropriate place settings. The chef had done it up right. Ted smiled at us both as we walked into the room and located our assigned seats. Once seated, the doors were closed and the meeting began. Ted was a skilled presenter and an accomplished speaker. He welcomed all of us, congratulated each person for their promotion, and sincerely thanked us for our contributions to the medical center and the communities we served. Next, Ted recapped his tenure with the medical center. He talked about what RMS was like when he first arrived. He spoke of the organization's need for a clear mission and a vision (the need for purpose) and how this team had all worked together to communicate the new mission and vision, making them a reality within the organization. He talked about the difficult times they worked through as a team while they struggled to turn the organization around and build what was, at that time, a nationally recognized and awarded health care system.

Ted continued: *"But there are storm clouds gathering on the horizon for the health care industry. Our struggles before were focused against other, local hospitals. This new threat is not from our competitors down the street or across the river, but from Washington, D.C. We will be facing an unprecedented increase in Medicare regulations. There is even talk of federal legislation that may change the competitive landscape of health care forever.* (The legislation Ted referenced would eventually become the Affordable Care Act.) *As a team, we have never faced this great of a threat to RMS's future. Meeting this new threat is one of the reasons we have expanded our leadership team to include four new members. We can no longer afford to think the same way as we have in the past. We must change in order to survive the storm that is coming. To do that, we need to think differently. One of the pitfalls of success is complacency. Many times leaders who have reached a certain level of success in their professional lives focus only on maintaining their current environment. They become unwilling to offer or even consider differing opinions. Leaders who become complacent have difficulty seeing future risks and miss out on new opportunities.*

"This is the best team of leaders anywhere. I will stack this group up against any leadership team. We will not allow ourselves to fall prey to complacency. As of today, we have four new leaders at the table. All of us must work together to face the storm on the horizon. Each of us must accept these new challenges with an open mind. I want you to ask questions, to challenge each other and the status quo. We can no longer afford to rest on our past successes. Now is the time for us to change RMS. Now is the time for us to prepare for the future.

"With that in mind, I want to show you a powerful message regarding the dangers of 'groupthink.' This video is a series of interviews and commentary by the engineers and leaders at NASA. This group worked on the tragic Challenger Shuttle mission. Their words touched me and I hope they speak to you as well."

With that being said, Ted encouraged us to eat our lunch while we watched the presentation, and after we finished our meal, we would discuss our thoughts. The video was about thirty minutes long, and as you can well imagine, it was truly a powerful message. After the video was over, Ted opened the discussion with an invitation for thoughts and comments from the group. All sat silent for a few moments, then Dan spoke. Dan's comments echoed Ted's words. First, he welcomed the new leaders. Then Dan congratulated those who were now *senior* leaders. He summarized his thoughts regarding the video and the challenges ahead by repeating parts of Ted's earlier comments. Dan referenced the storm clouds and recapped RMS's previous successes. He talked about how good the *senior* team was and that their success was rooted in their ability to reach consensus regarding how best to accomplish the tasks at hand. And finally, Dan told the group how pleased he was that I had assumed responsibility for the medical center's financial areas. My new role would free up some of his time so he could do more. He would be able to focus more on the acquisition of physician practices, which would help continue the rapid growth of the medical center.

While Dan was speaking, I was watching the faces of those seated at the table. Everyone was nodding their heads in collective agreement. Everyone but one, Ted. The CEO was providing no outward signs of agreement. When Dan was done, Ted thanked him for his comments, congratulated him for his successes, and called for more input from the group. The senior leaders took their respective turns in echoing Ted's perspective and confirming Dan's comments. As each person spoke, Ted's body language began to hint at his displeasure with what was being said. Finally, he turned to the four of us, the new members of the group, and called for our thoughts. Hank, being the most familiar with Ted, spoke for the group. He thanked Ted and the *senior* group for allowing us the opportunity to join the leadership team. He expressed how meaningful today's meeting had been and he was inspired to do more.

My fifty-year-old self sat silently, not because of anything Dan had said to me in our meeting before the meeting, but because experience had taught me that now was probably not the best time for me to speak. I agreed 100 percent with Ted's conclusion that there were serious storm clouds gathering on RMS's horizon. This pending storm was going to sweep over the entire health care system and we needed to get prepared. RMS needed to change drastically and rapidly. Also, based on years of leading change, I understood what it would take to move the medical center forward, and viewing a single video was only a small first step toward a much larger goal. I also had the feeling that Ted was a more talented leader than his senior group realized. I had listened to many stories told by those working in the trenches. Stories about how when Ted first came to the medical center, he was a constant fixture in the halls of the hospital. They talked about how he called each person by their first name and was constantly reminding them about who we were all working for: the patients, their families, and the communities we served. Ted was clearly a skilled leader of change and he understood the power which comes from purpose forming the foundation for change. During his first few years at the helm of RMS, the organization rediscovered their lost sense of pride in their mission. The RMS culture had reestablished purpose. Over the next few years, the medical center's growth was phenomenal. During this time, the organization's overriding strategic plan was "build it and they will come." In other words: "Serve more patients, offer more services, and do it through a network of more buildings." Or, if you really want to boil the strategic objective for RMS down, it was volume, volume, and more volume. There was no arguing with the success of this strategy. The signs of success were reflected in gleaming new buildings, cutting-edge patient services, and numerous national awards.

The leadership team had successfully implemented enough structure around change to reduce the chaos which had been caused by years of rapid growth. If some structure is good, more structure will be even better, right? And so it began. RMS's leadership layered on more and more structure in order to gain tighter and tighter control over their rapid expansion. As is always the case, the restrictions eventually reached the point where growth had begun to slow. The culture of DO had been firmly situated as the foundation for the medical center's process of change for some time. Ted sensed that the pendulum of purpose and structure had swung too far to the side of control. Now was the time to re-balance the organization. The question he faced was, is it even possible to re-balance the medical center, given the team he had assembled and the culture that he, himself, had supported for the last several years? Based on his reaction during this first meeting, I sensed that he was disappointed with the response of his leadership team. He had spent years teaching them to lead this way and now he expected them to change on a dime just because he sees some clouds on the horizon. Not a chance.

At the end of the meeting, Ted got up and handed out a book on change management to each of us. His instructions were for us to read the book and we would reassemble in two weeks for another special leadership meeting to discuss what we had learned. With that, the meeting was over. We had a great meal and the senior leaders had spent the balance of the ninety-minute meeting telling Ted what they thought he wanted to hear. The next two weeks passed quickly. The time had arrived for the second *special* meeting.

This second meeting was held in the evening with dinner being served for the assembled group. Ted opened the meeting by recapping his concerns for pending changes from Washington, D.C. He reiterated his faith in the senior leadership group and once again recounted their previous successes. When he finished his opening remarks, he stated that each of us would be given time to offer our thoughts regarding our takeaways from the book on change management. He wanted to hear from his senior leaders first, then from each of the four newcomers.

The first to speak was Dan. He summarized the content of the book as if he were giving a book report to the teacher. He was professional and concise. When Ted asked him if he found the book to be useful and what was his main takeaway from his reading, Dan replied that the ideas offered by the author would certainly help him do more each day. This time, Ted's body language was obvious from the very start. Each subsequent report echoed the tone set by Dan. With each *ditto* offered by the leaders, Ted appeared to become more and more frustrated. The CEO began to ask probing questions of each leader, which resulted in the same, standard, book report answers. As the evening progressed, Ted's frustration turned to despair. As time wore on, the meeting exceeded its ninety-minute allotment. Ted was seated at the head of the conference table and my assigned seat for the evening was at the opposite end of the table. I was the last to speak and it was clear that Ted was already mentally and emotionally out the door. Let's see if the timing is right for me to inject a different perspective.

I began my comments by saying: *"I may have missed the point of the book. I had a completely different take on the author's intent. As I read her message, I thought she was talking directly to me and to us as a group."* As I spoke those words, Ted's body language changed completely. He leaned forward, almost coming out of his chair, and responded: *"Exactly! Why did you think she was talking to us?"* I responded to Ted by recapping the sections of the book which were the most meaningful to me and the leadership experiences which made them personal. As I spoke, Ted came alive. At this point, he was showing signs of enthusiasm where, not ten minutes earlier, he was struggling to remain engaged. I spoke for less than five minutes. After I stopped speaking, there was dead silence in the room. The stares from most of the senior leadership team were ominous. Clearly, I had not *gotten the memo* instructing me to follow the accepted norm established by Dan and echoed by all the other leaders. Was I that stupid or was I some kind of free-thinking radical? In either case, clearly my having a seat at this table was a mistake which needed to be corrected or controlled as soon as possible.

Ted broke the silence by thanking the group for their time and their thoughts. He knew better than to call additional attention to me by publicly requesting a follow-up, one-on-one meeting. No one, other than Hank, spoke to me after the meeting. I was alone as I walked back to my office in administration. I knew exactly what I had done that evening. That's one of the many differences between Rob at thirty years old and Rob at fifty years old. I had intentionally separated myself from the culture of DO. I knew when I walked back to my office that there was a high probability that my career at RMS would be over within the next twenty-four months. Shoot, depending on Ted's reaction to my comments, my career may be over the next morning. Regardless of the ultimate outcome, at fifty I understood what needed to be done to effect the necessary changes. My only question was: Did Ted know what to do with what I had just offered? Most likely, I would have my answer in the morning.

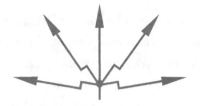

A conversation with the CEO – Part 1

Silence. That is what greeted me the following morning. The CFO was nowhere to be seen, and later that morning when his office door did finally open, there was no customary "Good morning" coming from the other side of the hall. No, silence was the order of the day. At around 10:30 that morning, I was seated at my desk with my head down working away when I heard a quiet rap on the frame of my office door, followed by *"Good morning"* spoken in a hushed tone. The CEO was standing in the doorway to my office. Although his office was only forty feet down the hall, this was the first time he had been to my office. Ted asked: *"Do you have a minute?"* *"Yes sir,"* I replied. *"Come see me,"* he said as he turned and started walking down the hall toward his office suite.

Over my lifetime, I have had the opportunity to spend time in some really nice executive offices. Ted's office was the most elaborate and finely appointed I had seen. It projected success, which was its intended purpose. Ted used his office as the meeting place for recruiting prominent physicians from all around the country. He needed them to see the success offered by relocating to our small corner of Kentucky. I followed Ted into his office and he closed the doors behind us. And yes, there were two large wooden doors which formed the entry into his office.

"Can I get you anything? Coffee? A water?" he asked. *"Yes sir. A water would be good. Thank you,"* was my answer. Ted pointed for me to sit in one of the chairs in front of his desk. He handed me a bottle of water

and sat down in the other chair beside me. *"Tell me about yourself. You've been here for two years now, but since your interview, we haven't really spent much time together. I've been told that you are a really talented bean counter, a creative 'fixer,' but I think there is way more to you than what I have been led to believe. Where did you grow up?"* And with that starting point being established, I gave Ted a verbal resume with heavy emphasis placed on my wide variety of leadership experiences, educational programs designed for executives and board members, experiences in leading cultural change, M&A, and a summary of my core believes (the three rules plus my personal *choices* and *needs*). If I was reading his intent correctly, he was searching for an internal human catalyst for change, someone to lead the process of change within the medical center. Time would tell.

A one-on-one meeting with Ted was typically limited to no more than thirty minutes. Also, Ted's time was always tightly scheduled, so his meetings were usually back to back, and almost always with senior staff and physicians as well as local, state, and federal community leaders/politicians. This first one-on-one meeting with Ted would run close to two hours. Coming out of this meeting were two main results.

First, during our meeting, his admin, Debbie, interrupted us to let Ted know that Dan, the CFO, and the SVP of HR were here for their 11:00 meeting and they were waiting to see him. Ted responded by instructing Debbie to tell them that he was in a meeting with Rob and they could reschedule their 11 o'clock for later that afternoon. It was at that very moment I knew the productive relationships with the members of the senior group which I had crafted over the last two years were, most likely, in need of serious repair or gone altogether. I had to believe that Ted knew what he had done as well. The CEO had just separated me from the other VPs.

RMS's structure was very clear. No VP would meet with Ted unless accompanied by the SVP they reported to. So, for example, proper protocol would be that Dan should have been present at this meeting in order to monitor (control) my input to the CEO. Ted had just cut through the rules, which he had helped to establish, and met with me one-on-one, without Dan. On top of that, the meeting had gone for more than just a few minutes. Who knows how much damage I could be causing? In the minds of the senior leadership team, an uncontrolled VP in an extended meeting with the CEO equated to unnecessary risk to the medical center's culture. Even worse, Ted gave a slap in the face to established structure when, knowing that Dan was waiting to see him for a scheduled meeting, Ted did not invite Dan to join us. But these side effects were of no concern to the CEO. They were my problems to deal with, not his.

You may have a couple thoughts running through your mind at this point. Thoughts like: "Surely the CEO didn't realize he was putting Rob into that position with the senior group," and "This meeting wasn't Rob's doing, it was Ted's meeting. That kind of a reaction from the senior group is pretty petty." Let's take them in order. First, keep in mind that Ted was an extremely skilled executive and a brilliant tactician. A few years my senior, he had spent his entire life in the health care industry and the last several years building RMS. Of course, he knew what he was doing. Most experienced executives have become very skilled at being *risk takers by proxy*. They are always willing to put others at risk, in this case me, in order to advance their agenda. I understood what he was doing because I had lived through it before, during my days at RB. My personal choice is not to lead in that manner. But, just because I choose to accept the risk myself doesn't mean that my way is always the best way. Owning the result happens to be right for me.

> *Most experienced executives have become very skilled at being risk takers by proxy. They are always willing to put others at risk in order to advance their agenda.*

Next, was the expected reaction from the senior group to be viewed as "petty" or vindictive in some way? Where these bad people? Answers: no and of course not. RMS had been under the thumb of the culture of DO for some time. Control was maintained through structure and the structure was meticulously documented and communicated through the use of policy, procedure, and detailed organizational charts. The rules governing my behaviors as a VP had been provided to me, in writing. In addition, I had gone through a required meeting with the SVP of HR to discuss, at length, RMS's expectations for me as a VP. My meeting with Ted was in direct violation of several long-standing and clearly communicated rules. I am sure that running through the minds of the senior group would be: "If I couldn't be trusted to adhere to the established structure, then what good am I to the group?"

Before you can develop the capacity to understand and respect someone else's perspective, you must understand your own. I had successfully led teams in both the culture of WHY and the culture of DO. My personal comfort zone is always centered on purpose, leading the WHY. But, Leadership Rule #3 requires me to maintain balance, and for that I have always taken the time to understand and respect the structure required by the culture of DO. The vast majority of the leaders you will encounter are creatures of structure. They are card-carrying members of the culture of DO. However, the successful leader is one who has developed the capacity for understanding both purpose and structure. I suspected that Ted was once firmly in the WHY camp and had spent his first few years at RMS driving purpose within the medical center. At some point along the way, Ted realized the need for balance and switched over to managing change through the implementation of structure. Now, what he had seen in me was a glimmer of purpose. He was testing to see how much I actually understood about the process of change. Which leads us to the second, most important result which came out of my first one-on-one with the CEO.

Early in our conversation, I touched on my prior experiences with leadership education. I explained my approach to leadership education.

I shared with him that over the last twenty years or so, my primary responsibility had been to build sustainable franchise value. During that time, I certainly enjoyed working with others and building companies, but I loved, and my passion is for building people. Some of the folks I have worked with went on to become leaders. Some would go on to become managers. My hope is that they all go on to become better people. When given the opportunity to teach, my goal is for the executives and front-line managers alike to learn to *live better and lead differently.*

This was the opening Ted had been hoping to discover. The moment I finished with my summary of leadership education, Ted said: *"Show me. Show me how you would teach leaders about change management."* I shot back: *"Sure. Do you mind if we go over to the conference table so I can draw a couple of illustrations?"* We moved to the other side of his office and sat down at a large conference table where I pulled out a notepad and began by drawing the Greek alphabet character Delta, the symbol for change. I labeled the triangle the "Culture of DO" and then summarized the characteristics of DO. Next, I drew the upside-down triangle on the same paper and placed it below DO and on the far right side of the page. This was labeled the "Culture of WHY." I proceeded to go through the characteristics commonly found in WHY. I tore this page out and placed it face up on the table in front of Ted.

On the clean sheet in front of me, I then drew the two cultures in alignment, but still separated. DO was at the top of the page and WHY was at the bottom. At this point, we talked about what must happen in order to effectively move the two cultures into alignment when preparing for change. Tearing off the second sheet and placing it beside the first sheet, face up in front of Ted, I used a third sheet to draw the two cultures coming into contact with each other, symbolizing the start of the actual process of change. I labeled this new illustration "The Plate Tectonics of Change" and launched into the concept of working in the trenches and the subduction zones of change. And finally, we talked about the impacts felt within the organization if DO formed the foundation for change vs. the expectations for change when WHY formed the foundation.

I can honestly say that I have never had a more engaged executive. Conceptually, Ted consumed these concepts as quickly as I could deliver them. His understanding grew with each new level. His questions were excellent and his grasp of the potential benefit for RMS was immediate. We were moving on to the next level when there was a second knock on his door. It was Debbie, again. This time, she was interrupting to remind Ted that he needed to catch a flight and if he didn't leave in the next fifteen minutes, he was going to be late.

"Thanks Debbie," Ted said as he turned back toward where I was seated. *"Rob, this is exactly what we need! Is there more of this?"* I answered: *"Yes sir, we are just getting started."* Ted stood up from the table and continued: *"Good! I am out of town for the next few days. I'll be back on Tuesday. If you were going to teach leadership to the entire RMS leadership council, what would that look like? That's what I want to see on Tuesday. Debbie will let you know when and where we'll meet Tuesday. Enjoy your holiday weekend. See you Tuesday. And Rob, keep this meeting between us for now. I know you understand why. Do you need these?"* Ted asked that last question as he was scooping up the three sheets of paper off the table and rolling them up to form a tube in his hand. With that being said, the CEO shook my hand and escorted me out of his office, closing the doors behind me.

I headed back down the hall to my office in a mild state of shock. What had just happened? Tuesday? Are you kidding me? This is Thursday afternoon. I have meetings scheduled for the rest of the afternoon. Tomorrow I was planning on heading home at noon and we are headed out of town to visit family over the holiday weekend. Ted was famous for placing this type of impossible demand on his direct reports. He would routinely ask for, and expect, the impossible. The leaders that made up his inner circle knew, all too well, about his tendency for issuing extraordinary demands and expectations. That was one of the reasons they were so insistent that no VP should be left alone, one-on-one with Ted for an extended period of time. Well, I was neck-deep in it now.

A few years ago, I had constructed in Freelance most of the materials I wanted to use in my Tuesday meeting with Ted. Freelance was the name of the presentation software inside of a PC-based package called Lotus. All of the PCs at the medical center were running on the Microsoft platform, exclusively. I was sure that what I had built could be converted from Freelance to PowerPoint, but my current set of skills did not include an in-depth understanding of PowerPoint. Late that afternoon, I spent a couple precious hours of time in a failed attempt to convert my previous work. Now what?

Time was ticking away and my options were limited. Long ago, I had taught myself the value of returning to a clean sheet of paper to solve difficult problems. I used that concept as a way of approaching this problem. Shoot, the hand-drawn illustrations I had just used worked fine in our earlier meeting, why not use hand-drawn illustrations for our Tuesday meeting? It would be completely different from what he was accustomed to seeing, which may help the information to stand out in his mind. This was a low-tech approach to a high-touch, people-centric project. I pulled out some blank printer paper, my plastic flowcharting template, and started constructing Tuesday's presentation.

I spent all day Friday in my off-campus office creating what I needed for my next meeting with Ted. Jennifer and I traveled over the weekend, as planned, and I finished the illustrations over the holiday. Tuesday morning, I made a copy of the materials and made some notes to myself in the margins of my copy. By eight o'clock, I was ready for the next meeting, which was scheduled for noon in a small conference room located in the hospital, away from the administrative building. At 11:45 that morning, I walked into an empty conference room, and organized my materials and my thoughts while waiting for the CEO to arrive.

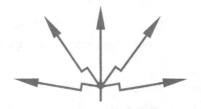

A conversation with the CEO – Part 2

The CEO entered the conference room about five minutes late. Ted was obviously in a hurry and he was in full boss mode. *"Okay, what have you got? I only have about thirty minutes, so let's make this quick,"* was the greeting from Ted as he glanced at his watch. I had been told to schedule the meeting for an hour. Time to improvise, moving on to Plan B. *"Understood. We can make that work. I know you are busy and I appreciate your time. Here is what we covered last Thursday,"* was my response. I proceeded to lay out in front of him the cleaned up versions of the three illustrations we had covered in our first meeting. I began the process of summarizing our last meeting. My objective was to bring the CEO back to the same level of engagement as when we ended our meeting four days earlier. I had been reviewing the materials for less than five minutes when Ted interrupted with: *"Yes, yes, I've got this. We covered this before. What else do you have?"* I looked at Ted for a couple of seconds, smiled, turned my presentation papers face down on the conference table, and walked over to the whiteboard. Time for Plan C. I am now creating the balance of this presentation based solely on prior experiences.

I wrote on the board as I spoke: *"There are three basic types of change: **Glacial, Purposeful,** and **Resulting**. All three types of change utilize the cultures of DO and WHY and follow the principles regarding the Plate Tectonics of Change."* Standing at the board, I pointed to each type of change and continued: *"**Glacial** change is slow-moving, but unstoppable change.*

It is inevitable change that everybody knows is coming. You can't stop or alter Glacial change, so the only option available is to anticipate its impact and adapt to its effects.

"Next is **Purposeful** *change. As the name implies, Purposeful change is change initiated for a specific reason. There are three types of Purposeful change:* **Strategic**, **Macro,** *and* **Micro***. Each type indicates a different level of intended scope. Strategic, Purposeful change is the broadest in scope, the most complex to implement, and has the longest duration. Think of a cultural transformation process as an example of Strategic. Macro, Purposeful change still contains a large scope, but it is more defined than Strategic. For example, if we strategically set out to transform the culture of the entire organization, the process of transforming the culture within those areas reporting to the CFO would be a Macro purpose. Changing the culture of those areas reporting to the SVP of HR would be another Macro purpose, etc. Micro, Purposeful changes are very defined and typically are completed on a much shorter time horizon. Continuing with my CFO example, Micro change would be the specific changes planned for the accounting area, hospital billing, or registration. A Micro change may be as narrow as the transformation of a single process within the accounting area. You get the idea. Below Micro, Purposeful changes are the actual tactics to be employed in order to accomplish the overall strategic objectives. Purposeful change: Strategic; Macro; and Micro.*

"This leads us to the remaining type of change, **Resulting***. This one is pretty self-explanatory. Think of Resulting change in terms of cause and effect. Resulting change is by far the easiest and quickest to implement, quantify, track, and trend.*

"Now, let's go back to our illustration where the cultures of DO and WHY are aligned and about to come into contact. Which culture is more suited for leading Resulting change?" Ted responded immediately with: *"DO."* I continued: *"Which culture is best suited for leading Purposeful change?"* Again, the CEO responded immediately with the correct answer: *"WHY."* I knew from his quick responses that Ted was fully engaged. It was time to take the presentation to the next level. I then asked:

"Where does the power reside in the culture of DO to implement Resulting change? Within DO, are Resulting changes initiated by executive leadership, those who reside in the narrow range at the top of the DO culture, or within this broad section at the bottom, the front-lines?" Before he could respond, I added: *"And, where within the culture of WHY does the power reside to effectively implement Purposeful change? At the broad leading edge of WHY or at the narrow bottom of the model?"* I leaned across the table, and using the illustration Ted was viewing, I pointed to the gap that existed between those at the top of DO who controlled Resulting change and those at the leading edge of WHY who will be implementing Purposeful change. I continued: *"The key to the successful implementation of any significant change is always held in two, separate locations. Those at the top of DO manage/control Resulting change and those on the leading edge of WHY are the leaders of Purposeful change. Look at the model. As the two cultures come into contact and the process of change begins, who within Do is closest to the purpose of change? The front-lines. Who within DO is the furthest from the purpose of change, but yet controls the structure surrounding the front-lines? The executive leaders. When the two cultures collide, those at the front-lines will naturally tend to adopt the new purpose because they are closer to it and will understand its value more rapidly than those at the top. Unless they are prepared well in advance and have accepted the value of the new purpose, those controlling the structure of DO will immediately put into place controls designed to slow or stop the process of change. This natural conflict between the two cultures, the Plate Tectonics of Change, creates friction all along the point of contact.*

"Substantive communication from the leaders of change, those on the leading edge of the new purpose, must be effectively targeted at both the executive team and the front-line leaders. This methodology is known as 'top-down and bottom-up' leadership. If we can effectively communicate the value of our new purpose to both groups, the culture of WHY will form the foundation of change. If we fail to effectively communicate the value of the new purpose, or we choose to communicate to only one of the two levels, DO will form the foundation of change."

At this point, we were well beyond our allotted time of thirty minutes. I stopped my presentation and standing next to the board, I asked: *"We are out of time; do you want to reschedule another meeting?"* Ted lifted his eyes off of the illustrations in front of him and said: *"What?... No, keep going. You were talking about the friction created by change and the value of using the top-down and bottom-up approach to change leadership."* For the next several minutes, we discussed the concepts of friction, trenches, subduction zones, and the use of buffers (objective and subjective). I wove into the conversation how the concepts behind top-down and bottom-up leadership would work within RMS. The CEO remained totally engaged. He asked great questions which showed me his natural level of curiosity and his capacity to understand and truly grasp these new concepts.

About ninety minutes into the meeting, Ted pushed the stack of paper that had been in front of him away and said: *"I see where you are going with this and it is exactly what we need. Now, how do you teach the new purpose to the senior leadership team and our front-line leadership group? The senior team needs to buy into the purpose before we roll this out to the front-lines. If we don't get them on board first, we'll create more friction than the organization can stand. And, how would you explain our new purpose? I figure you already have an answer. Is it in this stack of papers or are you going to put it up on the board?"* I glanced over at Ted and, without verbally responding to his last question, I stepped to the whiteboard and erased everything we had covered so far. This is the equivalent of getting out a clean sheet of paper. My fifty-year-old self knew that, at this point, we had passed beyond the *can you do it* phase and entered into the *how will you do it* phase.

On the left-hand side of the blank board, I wrote: *pure form of DO = structure and results*, and below that line, I wrote *pure form of WHY = freedom and results*. Then I turned to Ted and said: *"We know that neither culture can exist in its pure form for an extended period of time. DO's structure will ultimately squash results through ever-increasing restrictions implemented to gain and maintain complete control. WHY's freedom, left unchecked by the application of structure, will result in chaos, making innovation impossible. The common denominator for the two cultures of change centers on* **results**.*"* I circled the word *results* in both lines and then wrote *Results* in the center of the board.

I continued: *"This is how we begin educating both the executive team and our team members at the front-lines. Both RMS groups have been taught to value the ability to produce the desired results. This is the common denominator for both cultures and provides us with common ground to build on, even though their perceptions surrounding results are at polar opposites. The front-lines have been taught to place the highest value on the results surrounding patient outcomes, and rightly so. The executive team values patient outcomes, but they see results in terms related to the entire organization's performance. The key point is both have been taught to place a high value on accomplishing results, however they may be defined.*

"This is where we begin. We will start by modifying the perception of results within the two groups. We will establish a commonly shared understanding for desired results. In short, Ted, we teach each set of leaders a new language. They will be learning the vocabulary of change, which consists of new illustrations, terminology, and definitions. You already have the first part of the vocabulary in front of you, the cultures of DO and WHY, Plate Tectonics of Change, friction, etc. Now, let's take understanding of this new vocabulary to the next level. This next illustration is where both sets of leaders will immediately grasp the benefits generated by Purposeful change."

At this point, I drew on the board a vertical line to the right of the word Result and said: *"Results are the y-axis."* Using a point of origin at the base of the y-axis, I drew a horizontal line and labeled this axis as Time. *"And Time forms the x-axis."* I then turned to the CEO and said: *"Using this simple coordinate grid, we have established a meaningful way to discuss the process of change with both groups. We are now teaching the vocabulary of change. We begin by teaching both groups to think of it not as change, but rather as 'Results over Time.' Now we have created a link to both sides through the use of Results. We know that every RMS team member is familiar with the importance of results. We also know that everyone has an appreciation for the value of time. With this foundation being established, we can layer on the next step in teaching the concept of purposeful change."* I turned back to the board and drew a dotted line, starting about three-fourths of the way up the Results axis and running parallel to the Time axis. Next, I drew a second dotted line. This line began about one-fourth of the way up the Results axis and ran parallel to Time. Illustration #4 below shows the graph's development, so far.

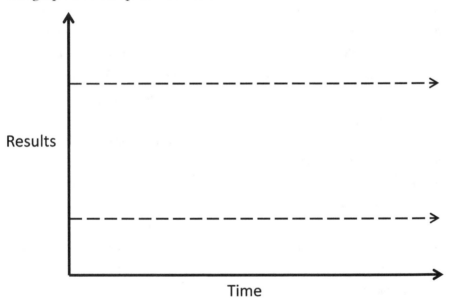

I turned around to assess Ted's willingness to continue. At this point, he was leaning back in his chair with both feet propped up on the conference table. Had I lost him or was he enjoying the presentation? He knew why I had paused and immediately responded to me with: *"Keep going. I am following. I want to see where you are going with this."* *"Yes sir. Thank you. How am I on time?"* I asked. *"Fine. What's next?"* were my instructions from the CEO. I turned back to the whiteboard and continued to expand on the model being constructed to illustrate *Results over Time.* First, I labeled the top dotted line as *Acceptable.* Then, I labeled the lower dotted line as *Unacceptable.* Once the two lines were labeled, I continued with my explanation of the model: *"The top dotted*

line indicates the point at which the Result reaches the threshold of being Accept-able. Once deemed as Acceptable, the organization no longer needs to allocate additional resources toward attaining the desired Result. The key concept is for everyone to understand what is meant by Acceptable Results. Acceptable to whom? Are the results acceptable to the patient? The patient's family? The team member's immediate supervisor? Or, are they acceptable to the executive leadership team because they fall within a range defined by a policy? Do they meet an established strategic objective which is known to the executive level, but not by the front-line? Answering these questions is absolutely necessary if the two groups are to establish a shared understanding of the new purpose. The way we teach others to assess acceptability is through the use of various facilitation techniques, the use of commonly known tools like the Five Whys, and the use of standard leadership concepts like PDCA, Plan Do Check Act." Ted had been silent for a while, but at this point he interjected: *"Finally, something I am familiar with. I understand the use of facilitation, the Five Whys, and PDCA. Keep going."* I responded with: *"Yes sir. Thank you. The exact same questions and techniques are applied as we grow to understand the reasoning behind the lower threshold, the Unacceptable level* of Results.

"Here is how the Results over Time model works. Pick a topic or a task. Any topic or task works the same within the model. We can apply the Results over Time model if the target task is delivering meals to patients or improving utilization percentages for the Operating Rooms. Regardless of the topic or task, the basic concepts for the model are unchanged, only the scales used on the axis change to accommodate the measurement of the Result. Likewise, the anticipated length of the Time needed to accomplish the task will be adjusted to match the topic. The third variable is how narrow is the gap between a Result becoming Acceptable vs. Unacceptable?

"Let's say that the task selected by the group for discussion, the Result, has a current success rate of 25 percent. The group has determined that a 25 percent rate is Unacceptable. (I wrote 25 percent on the Results axis as a way to mark the value assigned to the point of origin for the lower dotted line.) *The group then establishes that an Acceptable Result would be a success rate of 75 percent.* (I wrote 75 percent on the Results axis as a way to

mark the value assigned to the point of origin for the upper dotted line.) *Now we turn our attention to the x-axis, the perception of Time needed to affect the necessary improvements. We know that the group says we are at an Unacceptable success rate of 25 percent today.* (I labeled the point of origin for the Time axis as 'Today'.) *My next question to the group would be: 'How long do you think it will take RMS to reach an Acceptable success rate of 75 percent?' Let's say their answer, after what is usually a considerable amount of discussion, is three months.* (I went out about halfway on the Time axis and drew a small circle, labeling it three months. I then drew a star along the Acceptable line, placing it directly above the three months label on the Time line.) *Once we have established which Result over Time needs to be improved and we have determined an expected period of time for that improvement to take place, the future vision for the group is beginning to form. All that remains is to establish our interim progress goals for month one and month two and, most importantly, we will be defining the resources needed to accomplish an Acceptable Result.*

"Just for this example, let's assume that the ramp-up time follows a normal pattern for a short-term, Purposeful change such as this. The first few weeks are typically spent in the planning phase of PDCA. During the planning phase, we may see a slight increase in the success rate simply because team members are talking about it more and the leaders are paying closer attention to the Result. As we enter the Do phase of PDCA, if our plan was well conceived, we will see a dramatic increase in the success rate of the Result until we meet or exceed the established Acceptable level. This line, which looks like the leading edge of a bell curve, reflects our progress toward correcting the Result. However, and most importantly, this line also represents the amount of **resources** *being expended by RMS to implement the Result over Time. Resources. This term is another addition to the vocabulary of change. We need to learn to be thinking about the resources being expended and the costs being incurred in order to generate an Acceptable Result, the benefit. RMS is large, but our resources are finite. Therefore, the allocation of our limited resources must be an important part of everybody's thought process as we balance out cost vs. benefit."* See Illustration #5 below.

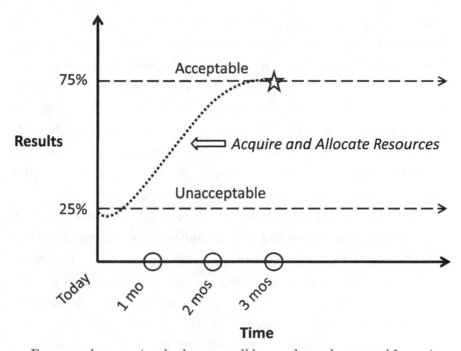

By now, the meeting had gone well beyond two hours and I was just getting warmed up when the CEO interrupted: *"I've seen enough. Am I right to assume there is a bunch more to be covered?"* *"Yes sir. I am just getting into the good stuff,"* I responded. Ted continued: *"I figured. Here is what I want. I want you to work with Janet, the director of training and education, to develop a presentation around the basics of change based on the book I had you read. You can use your three types of change, but stick mostly to the book for this first meeting. Then, I want you to work with Janet to develop an in-depth program for the entire leadership council based on what you have shown me here today. I want you to put together a program using everything you have used before to teach leaders."* I interrupted Ted, which I should not have done, to explain: *"There are three sections: Relationships, Culture, and Change. Do you just want me to focus only on change?"* The CEO was in full boss mode when he responded with: *"What did I just say? I want a program that contains everything. Once you are ready, I want to review the full presentation, slide by slide, concept by concept before anyone else sees it. Spread it out over a series of meetings with me. Each meeting is to last no more than an hour.*

Understood? By the way, all of this stuff is brilliant, perfect for what we need to accomplish. But, it doesn't mean anything if you and I are not on the same page. Do you know what our new purpose must become?" I turned back to the whiteboard and wrote one word: VALUE. I turned back around to face Ted and said: *"We have become masters at processing volume. We must now master the concepts around delivering value to every patient, family member, provider, and community we serve."* Those words brought a smile to the CEO's face, and as he walked briskly toward the door, he ended the meeting by saying: *"You got it. Now, figure out how we make it happen."*

With that, Ted was out the door and on to his next meeting. I sat down in the empty room and took a moment to gather my thoughts. What popped into my mind was: "Here we go again!" His acceptance of the material and his grasp of the concepts went well beyond what was anticipated. For myself, I had just created an opportunity that would challenge me, beyond anything I had faced before. The new opportunity was an exciting prospect. I was, once again, going to have the opportunity to teach, to help grow other leaders. It doesn't get much better, assuming that the leaders of DO wished to grow.

Over the next eighteen months, the educational process would go through many phases. As with any project of this complexity and scope, there are good days and those that are not so good. *Two steps forward and one step back.* As long as you are making progress, it is a good day. Anytime you are leading Purposeful change, where purpose is attempting to wrestle the foundation from established structure, you will be the target of strong emotions. The vast majority of those on the front-lines will welcome you, hanging on your every word, because the purpose you represent will align with their needs.

Those managing change from the upper regions of structure will have one of two reactions to your efforts. First, if the CEO's words and actions align in support of purpose, most of the managers of change will be passive-aggressive toward the new purpose. Their words will appear to support the process of change, but their actions will carry a stronger message of resistance. When viewed from the perspective of the next layer of managers, actions will always speak louder than words. The only way to successfully break this cycle of passive-aggressive resistance is to alter the mix of the executive team. For example, recall that I went to the technical conference in April by myself. RB's **new** CIO did not go with me because he had not been employed long enough to have his feet on the ground. Mr. E had taken a strong action which supported his words. He only needed to take this type of action once to alter the rest of the executive team's attitude toward RB's new purpose.

The second reaction will occur if the CEO's words and actions do not align in support of purpose. In this case, all of the managers of change will sense the lack of commitment and openly work to defeat the process of change. When this environment exists, anyone located below the CEO on the org chart, and deemed as a threat to the status quo will be removed from the organization in short order (days or weeks). If you are a Subjective Buffer (EHC or IHC) in this environment, working on the side of WHY, start packing your bags because you're DOne. Once the removal is accomplished, this action sends the strongest message possible to the front-lines: "Your purpose is to DO!" Purposeful change will now be defined by existing structure and any resulting success is limited to incremental improvement, only.

I survived for eighteen months after assuming the role of internal human catalyst within RMS. Based on what you have read in Life Lesson II: (1) Was there a moment where the CEO took personal ownership of the new purpose?; (2) Did the CEO's actions indicate his return to the culture of WHY or do you think he remained a member of the culture of DO?; and (3) Of all the illustrations I presented to the CEO during our two meetings, which one do you believe was the most impactful with the executive team and why? These three questions form the first part of the Epilog for Life Lesson II. Once we have answered these questions, we will complete our discussion of the Results over Time model and close out our journey by constructing the foundational model for all change, the Capacity for Understanding model. Now, on to our final section: Did the CEO ever take ownership of the new purpose?

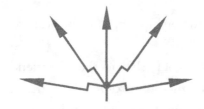

Epilog for Life Lesson II

<u>Was there a moment where the CEO took personal owner-ship of the new purpose?</u> Answer: No. Ted never had that reflective *moment of capitulation*, meaning he was unwilling to accept that his leadership had created a set of unsustainable conditions within RMS. Remember from Life Lesson I when Mr. E stared down at his cup of coffee and said, in a hushed tone: "My fault." Ted never took that level of personal ownership for the current result; therefore, he was not going to personally own/ lead the new purpose. A creative thinker and strategic leader possessing a high level of communication skills, Ted had earned his rewards and had every reason to avoid the obvious risks inherent in facilitating this level of cultural change. An executive who is an accomplished *risk-taker by proxy* will very rarely allow themselves to be placed in a position to own future, unknown results. A *risk-taker by proxy* will always construct a layer of plausible deniability which will allow

> *An executive who is an accomplished risk-taker by proxy will very rarely allow themselves to be placed in a position to own future, unknown results.*

them to deflect ownership should the future, unknown results become negative.

My fifty-some-year-old self had the experience to understand my role as the designated *risk-taker* from early in the RMS change process. Experience had also taught me that in order for us to have any chance at successfully installing WHY as the foundational culture within RMS, the CEO's words and actions needed to align in support of the new purpose. This leads us to our second question.

Did the CEO's actions indicate his return to the culture of WHY or do you think he remained a member of the culture of DO? Answer: The answer is twofold. Yes, in the beginning, the CEO did return to a position of leading RMS's process of change. Ted was clearly RMS's champion for new purpose. Then, as time went on, friction began to develop and circumstances evolved to a point where the CEO's words supported the new purpose, but his actions were decidedly supportive of structure. Ultimately, the CEO chose to remain a member of the culture of DO.

About three months into the change process, I had been promoted to RMS's VP and chief innovation officer. My office was now the first door on the right after you left the CEO's office suite. I had begun various coaching exercises with each member of the executive team, including coaching the CEO. At this point, we were about halfway through the process of designing the leadership education classes for both the executive team and the front-line leadership groups. We had already presented our initial education program regarding the process of change to the entire leadership council. The CEO was still fully engaged in the educational process and was out-front *promoting* the process of change. Notice that I didn't say he was *leading* the process of change. The words used by a CEO when *promoting* or *leading* the change process are very similar. The actions taken by someone *promoting* change are slightly different than the actions taken by someone *leading* change. Just that subtle difference between the two may be all that is needed to encourage the culture of DO to stand firm because: *this too shall pass.*

Below the surface, within the *senior* leadership team, friction was building. The friction took the form of consensus which equated to forced compliance and agreement. All of the senior leaders complied with the instructions they had been given. They dutifully attended the educational sessions as mandated by the CEO. Each senior leader faithfully invited me to the one-on-one meetings with their direct reports and accurately parroted the vocabulary of change. They were all complying with the tasks which had been assigned by the CEO. What was wrong? Answer: There was no ownership. No sense of urgency. The senior leaders possessed no emotional need for the new purpose.

However, spend a few hours with the leaders located within the lower levels of RMS's org chart, from the director level all the way to the front-line managers, and you would discover just the opposite perception of change. The vast majority of non-executive leadership embraced the process of change because they possessed a burning need for new purpose. Not only did they readily accept ownership of the change, they understood the fundamental need for new purpose and they perceived the value it represented. The further down the org chart you progressed, the closer to the trenches you went, the more passionate the response from the leaders. This split, the difference between *promoting change through consensus* and *leading change through ownership* is frequently the root cause of friction when the two cultures of change collide.

> *The difference between promoting change through consensus and leading change through ownership is frequently the root cause of friction when the two cultures of change collide.*

The most effective method for reducing change-related friction is to simultaneously *lead* the process of change from both the top-down *and* the front-lines-up. In RMS's case, Ted needed to commit to leading the change process, just as Mr. E assumed the responsibilities of leadership within RB. As you know from Life Lesson I, Mr. E experienced the moment of capitulation where he accepted ownership of the future result. His executive leadership team was dutifully promoting the process of change right up to the point where RB's chief information officer was terminated, followed shortly by the removal of the VP of IT. Effectively, Mr. E removed the old IT leadership team and replaced it with a completely new team. The new CIO was from outside of RB and outside of the banking industry, which served to further underscore Mr. E's message of Purposeful, Strategic change.

> *The most effective method for reducing change-related friction is to simultaneously lead the process of change from both the top-down and the front-lines-up.*

These actions taken by Mr. E were necessary if RB was to successfully adopt the changes needed to leverage technology, pushing it out and into the hands of the POS, resulting in enhanced value to the customer. His actions were in alignment with his words. The message Mr. E chose to send was consistent and unmistakably clear. He owned this process, the risks were his, and the rewards were directed toward others, specifically RB's CORE (customers, shareholders, and culture). As CEO, only he could effectively send this message, and once understood, the perceptions held by the top-down and front-line-up leaders were aligned. The culture of WHY, the new purpose, carried the heaviest weight and was going to form the foundation of RB's change process. Mr. E was leading change from the top-down and from the front-lines-up, and as a result, friction was reduced.

As a thirty-year-old leader, I was learning. As a fifty-year-old leader, it was my responsibility to teach by tactfully delivering the benefit of my prior experiences to RMS's CEO. This was the complex and politically charged topic on my agenda when I entered Ted's office and closed the door behind me. In my hand were two different versions of a proposed senior leadership development timeline. Along with the timeline, I also carried two differing versions of an RMS org chart showing suggested changes to the CEO's senior leadership team.

When I entered Ted's office, he was seated behind his desk and ready for another educational session related to the process of change. I began the meeting by asking his permission to discuss what may be a difficult subject. After giving his permission to continue, he relocated himself from behind the desk and settled into the chair beside me. This was a clear indication of his willingness to receive whatever was on my mind as a peer, not CEO to one of his direct reports. I proceeded to relay a brief version of my experiences with leading change within RB. We discussed the similarities of the two organizations. We talked about the almost identical wording used to express their visions, the *storm clouds gathering on the horizon*. Ted and I spent a few minutes reviewing the similarities between the personalities and characteristics of the two executive leadership teams. Then, with the background being established, I laid the two timelines down on the desk in front of us.

The first timeline showed my completing the leadership education process and stepping away from RMS in three months, leaving the leadership of the change process in Ted's more than capable hands. The second timeline showed my stepping away from RMS within the next twenty-four months, after completing the leadership education and the related change processes. This second timeline also showed Ted taking ownership of the new purpose, but after the culture of WHY had been established as the foundation for change. The second version called for specific actions to be taken by the CEO, meant to demonstrate his ownership, within the next three to four months. It also listed more actions to be taken by the CEO within the next nine months. What those specific recommendations were is not relevant to the story. What is relevant is Ted immediately grasped the critical nature of taking the proposed actions in order to affect top-down and front-line-up leadership, thereby reducing friction within the organization. Once he was presented with the two options, he focused only on the twenty-four-month timeline. We discussed, in detail, the organizational chart I had prepared in support of the longer option. At the end of the meeting, Ted scooped up both sets of documents, put them in his top desk drawer, and requested a more detailed leadership development plan for his executive team, given the modifications we had discussed. All in all, the meeting went as well as I could have hoped.

Over the next few months, Ted's actions and words aligned with the Purposeful, Strategic changes we had discussed. We had several more detailed follow-up meetings which focused on the senior leadership team and their role in *leading* the process of change, not just *promoting* it. About six months of the twenty-four-month timeline had passed when circumstances developed which clearly called for a change to be made within the senior team. Ted and I discussed the options and considered the downstream effects from the proposed change. He decided it was time to make the change, for the good of the organization and in support of the change process. A week passed and nothing happened. Two weeks, then a month went by and still no action. By the end of the second month of waiting for the action to occur, I realized that Ted's position on the proposed action had changed. In his mind, the risks related to making the senior leadership change had become too great. In my mind, Ted was unwilling to step outside of the structures established by the culture of DO in order to lead the new purpose. It was at this point I understood that my career within RMS was, most likely, limited to no more than another twelve months.

Once I understood Ted's course of action, I altered my definition of success for my role within the RMS change process. Please know that I was, out of respect, completely transparent with the CEO on what impact his choices would have on the process of change, my future effectiveness in leading the process, and the residual, negative impact this course of action would have on RMS's culture. Ted understood and did what he could to support me in my efforts to minimize the impact from RMS's culture of DO forming the foundation for the new purpose.

You may be asking yourself: "What happened to alter the CEO's path toward the culture of WHY? Who was proven to be right?" Here is another opportunity to learn about the awesome power of perception. My perceptions were all based on a specific set of facts which I thought were complete. For the first several months of this process, I did possess a complete set of facts which enabled me to help design effective strategic solutions for the benefit of RMS. During this period, the process was progressing smoothly. But, using the clarity of twenty-twenty hindsight, I would later learn that the facts had changed about six months into the process. Due to the confidential nature of these new facts, the CEO was unable to share them with me. Given the nature of the new facts, Ted's choices were understandable.

Based on my incomplete set of facts, I perceived Ted's most recent actions to be inconsistent with his prior actions and his current words. My fifty-something-year-old self knew, based on previous experiences, that circumstances change and that, unless I was in the role of CEO, I would not always be in possession of all the facts. This was very similar to the choices made by SBB's chairman from Life Lesson I. In the short term, the path chosen by the leader restricted the possible benefits to incremental improvements only. In the long term, given the perspective offered by the passage of time, SBB's chairman was proven correct.

Given the benefits offered by experience, I understood my new role within RMS. The definition of success for me had now changed. Success was no longer cultural transformation to embrace the new purpose, but rather to identify those I could help to grow in the short term and teach them what I could during my remaining time as RMS's internal human catalyst. Where would I find these leaders, the people I could help? Answer: in the trenches and the subduction zone. I was now in a position of leading the process of change from the front-lines-up. The possibility of installing WHY as the foundational culture at RMS had slipped away. My scope had narrowed, but my purpose was the same. I set out to find those willing to learn and help them to grow as individuals and as leaders.

Of all the illustrations I presented to the CEO during our two meetings, which one do you believe was the most impactful with the executive team and why? Answer: By far, the most impactful model for the executive team was the Results over Time model. We will discuss why this model was so relatable in a moment. But, let's first understand why the models for the cultures of change were viewed by the executive team as holding little value.

On the surface, one may think that the executive team would naturally relate to the broader, more strategic concepts found within the interactions between the two cultures of change, WHY and DO. Well, they didn't. Their rationale for dismissing the value of the model is very common among a successful group of leaders. The executive team acknowledged the validity of the theory, but rejected that its purpose, the WHY, had any major role in RMS's process for future change. After all, every team member had been tested for their ability to recite from memory RMS's mission and vision statements. Each team member had a job description complete with specific job tasks and responsibilities. They had each been given a handbook filled with policies and procedures, complete with a very specific disciplinary schedule for any violation of the established rules. No sir, there was no need for any new ideas, and if a new idea happened to be needed, the executive team would develop it, then pass it along to others for implementation. No one below the senior level needed to ask "why" because they already had the answer to their question, just look it up in the employee handbook. Or, if you couldn't find it in the handbook, just ask one of the executive team and they will tell you why. New purpose? Innovation? Going around looking at things in a new way? Are you kidding? Ridiculous, just look at all we have accomplished. How can you even suggest that there needs to be a second, balancing culture of purpose? The culture we have is working just fine, thank you very much.

The reactions listed above are all normal. As I have said before, these people were all extremely intelligent, very knowledgeable in their respective areas, high energy, skilled, and accomplished professionals.

They were good people, working very hard to accomplish the tasks they had been assigned, with the best of intentions. They also shared a single point of perspective: DO.

On the other side of the coin, the front-line leaders held a completely different perspective. These leaders embraced the concepts around the two cultures of change. They immediately recognized the forces of DO and the need for the balance of WHY. From the moment I put the triangles up on the screen, the front-line leaders engaged in meaningful conversation. These were the folks that lived and worked in the trenches. Every day, they dealt with the friction, and even though they didn't know how to express it in leadership terminology, they sure knew what it felt like. Every one of them could give me example after example of how RMS could change to improve the patient's experience or the organization's performance. Once again, we witness the power of perspective.

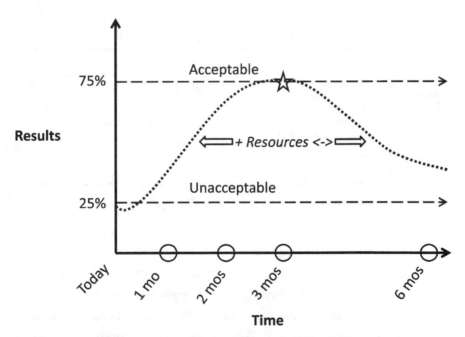

The one illustration that all the RMS leaders embraced was the Results over Time graph. The concepts contained within this graph resonated from the top-down and the front-lines-up, but as you may suspect, for different reasons. See Illustration #6 above. This is the illustration I had drawn on the whiteboard for Ted when he decided that he had seen enough.

Do you recall how we illustrated the allocation of resources over a period of time and the benefits gained through discussing Acceptable and Unacceptable levels of performance? Remember how we were building a new vocabulary for change? What you are about to see are the next steps in the application of the Results over Time model. These are the more complete graphs that were used as part of the leadership educational process. As we layer on additional concepts, be thinking about where in the educational process you believe each leadership group began to relate to the model.

See Illustration #7 below. This is the next step in building the Results over Time model.

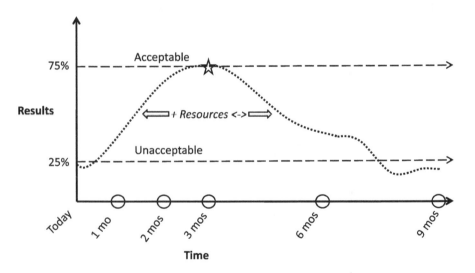

What you are seeing here is the graphic illustration of what almost always happens to an improvement implemented within the culture of DO. Notice the rapid increase in resources thrown at the problem in order to attain an Acceptable Result. This is the typical workflow associated with the *find it and fix it* mentality which is prevalent in DO. In this environment, achieving the goal is directly proportional to the allocation of additional resources assigned to fix the problem. Success is nothing more sophisticated than more attention being paid to a problem plus more costs being incurred in order to fix it. Now, notice the decline in Results, and the corresponding reduction in resources which takes place over Time after an Acceptable Result has been achieved. Ignore the actual scale used for Time in this illustration. It is just there as an example. The scale of Time related to a Result can be as short as hours or as long as years. What is important to note is the decline in the quality of the Result, post-success.

Why does this decline occur? Answer: the *find it and fix it* mentality within the structure of DO is built solely on accomplishing an assigned task, not on the need to achieve a purpose. Once the task is accomplished, the culture of DO demands that resources be reallocated to the next issue that has been assigned a higher priority. Since the origin of success for this Acceptable Result was a function of accomplishment, through increased resource allocation, the decline in the Result will reflect the reduction in allocated resources. This is a classic example of Resulting Change, cause and effect. Now we have completed the Results over Time cycle within the culture of DO. It now reflects the *"find it fix it and forget it"* mentality.

As Results decline and resources are diverted to the next priority, notice the extended period of Time the Results linger below the Unacceptable line. When Results return to the Unacceptable level, they appear to languish at the new lows for a period of at least a month. Here is why this pattern of delay is common. Once the threshold for an Unacceptable Result is breached, again, there will be a delayed response in the reallocation of resources, causing the quality of the Result to dip even lower than the original Unacceptable levels. The delayed response is caused by leadership's shock and dismay over the task's return to an Unacceptable level. The time lost in responding to the issue will be spent by upper management engaged in a fruitless effort to determine who was at fault for the return to an Unacceptable level of Result. After all, they fixed this problem once before. Someone needs to be held accountable for this current mess, and the only thing upper management knows for certain is this failure wasn't their fault. They will, no doubt, be spending precious Time discussing the following: "I'll bet if we change a policy or put in a new procedure, that will keep it from going bad again after we fix it this one last time." How familiar is this to you? Most all of us experience some version of this leadership mentality every day.

At this point in the education process, *all* of the front-line leaders grasped the concepts of the Results over Time model. They viewed it as an accurate representation of their daily lives and a graphic illustration of their daily frustrations. The top-down leadership group also accepted this model, but they perceived it very differently. The senior group saw the model as additional justification for their implementation of more structure. They literally looked at the illustration and said: "So that is why we have to spend all of our time fixing things." There are times that, even after all my years teaching this stuff, I am left scratching my head in wonder.

This next level of the Results over Time model is the one that really hit home with the senior group. Once I showed them Illustration #8 below, they adopted the model immediately. Next, they set about using it to support their need for the creation of additional layers of leadership beneath them so they could become more efficient at assigning tasks.

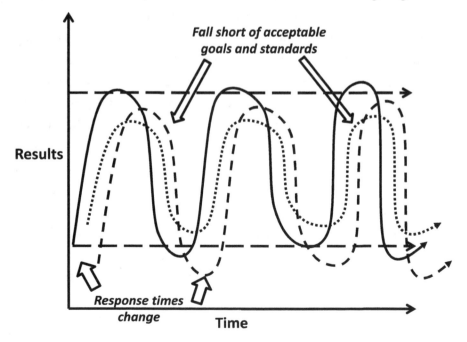

The intended value of this version of the Results over Time model is not to help senior leadership with justifying more layers of bureaucracy. This model's value is its ability to illustrate the reality of daily life in leadership. No leader is faced with only a single, high priority issue to resolve. Leaders are constantly juggling multiple priorities while simultaneously managing several different resource allocation processes. Because there are only so many hours in the day, and available resources are always limited, leaders are constantly making decisions based on the premise of *how good is good enough*. This is especially true within a rapidly growing organization. What you are seeing in Illustration #8 above is a simple representation of too much to do and not enough time in which to get it all done. This overwhelming wave density reflects the inevitable result created by the repeated application of a process known as *problem resolution*.

The process of *problem resolution* is best represented by using the form of a wave. *Problem resolution* waves have amplitude, height, which indicates the distance between an Acceptable Result and an Unacceptable Result. In addition to the level of Result, amplitude represents the allocation of additional resources needed to fix the problem or the redistribution of resources in order to fix a different, higher priority issue. *Problem resolution* waves also have frequency, length, which indicates the gap in time between reoccurring peaks (successes) and valleys (failures) within the change process for the task being addressed. When operating under the culture of DO, the leader capable of juggling the most tasks with the fewest *discoverable* failures is celebrated as the most skilled leader.

> *When operating under the culture of DO, the leader capable of juggling the most tasks with the fewest discoverable failures is celebrated as the most skilled leader.*

When the culture of DO forms the foundation for change, *problem resolution* is the acceptable method used to implement all aspects of authorized, incremental improvement within the existing structure. This series of illustrations, #5 through #8, is the visual representation of why change occurring within the foundation of DO will always result in incremental improvement. The new *problem resolution* waves created by the process of change, based within the culture of DO, are placed into competition for available resources along with all the other priority tasks. Guided by the perspective of the culture, change is perceived as just another task to be accomplished. Under the restrictive structure of DO, incremental improvement is the best result possible.

There is an alternative version of this model. The culture of WHY is based on freedom and results. Part of the freedom offered by the culture of WHY is created through the use of *solution design* as opposed to DO's use of *problem resolution*. *Solution design* can also be illustrated using the Results over Time model. See Illustration #9 below.

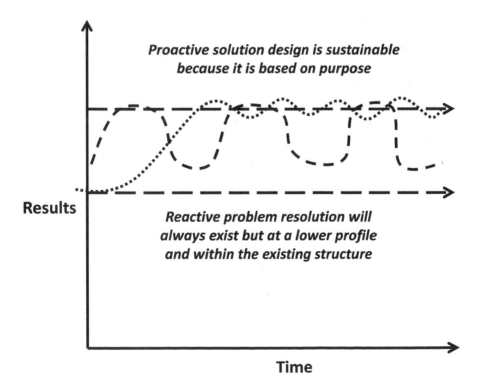

Proactive solution design is sustainable because it is based on purpose

Results

Reactive problem resolution will always exist but at a lower profile and within the existing structure

Time

Solution design is constructed using the same elements as *problem resolution*. It just prioritizes them differently. We still need to use facilitation to identify the Purposeful-Strategic Change and its Acceptable and Unacceptable Result levels. The process of change will follow the same Plan Do Check Act methodology and its resolution will still require the allocation of limited resources. When you boil it all down, the difference between *solution design* and *problem resolution* is *solution design* is founded on the need to accomplish a purpose, whereas *problem resolution* is based on the need to accomplish a result. Those working within the discipline of *solution design* will always begin their discussion of change with two questions: "Why are we making this change?" and "How will it benefit our customers, shareholders, and culture (the CORE of every organization)?" Answering these two foundational questions requires a much higher level of understanding on the part of the participants, especially during the Plan and Act stages of the PDCA process.

> *The difference between solution design and problem resolution is solution design is founded on the need to accomplish a purpose, whereas problem resolution is based on the need to accomplish a result.*

Notice that the *solution design* Results curve shown in Illustration #9 above begins with a much longer period of Time spent with minimal improvement in the Results and the allocation of only a few additional resources. This flat section of the curve indicates the investment of Time spent by those leading change in order to first understand the contemplated change. Understanding forms the foundation for all transformational leadership (a central theme from Book Two) and the capacity for understanding is the subject of our next section of Book Three.

Once the foundational questions of *solution design* are addressed, and a preliminary understanding of the task's purpose is obtained, the two curves take on a similar appearance. There will be a steep, upward slope reflecting the improved Results as additional resources are dedicated toward fixing the problem. The appearance of the two slopes may be similar, but the intended purpose of the additional resources is radically different. Within the process of *problem resolution,* resources are delivered with the stated goal of fixing the failure. Once the Acceptable Result is accomplished, everyone involved in the process of *problem resolution* expects the resources will be reassigned. Within the process of *problem resolution,* there is no sense of ownership. Under the process of *solution design,* resources are delivered with the stated goal of creating and maintaining the solution. Those implementing the change understand their purpose and they step up to own the Results.

> *Within the process of problem resolution, resources are delivered with the stated goal of fixing the failure and there is no sense of ownership.*

This brings us to the most obvious difference between the two Results over Time models. Once the targeted Results are achieved under *solution design,* they are maintained. Notice that the Results will fluctuate over Time, but the amplitude of the wave is contained within a much narrower band. This indicates the consistent delivery of higher quality Results to the CORE. The resulting innovations, generating enhanced

> *Under the process of solution design, resources are delivered with the stated goal of creating and maintaining the solution and the results are owned.*

sustainable value to the CORE, are created by the front-line leaders and supported by senior leaders. *Solution design* places the necessary understanding and authority to act in the hands of the leaders closest to the POS (point-of-service). There is no longer a protracted delay in the Act portion of the PDCA process as those implementing change in the trenches seek guidance and permission from those in control of the structure.

For senior leadership, those ultimately responsible for the consolidated Results of the organization, to effectively manage risk under a *solution design* model, they must have confidence in the Check portion of the PDCA process. Measurements must be timely and meaningful. Within *solution design* understanding, the Check portion is actually more important than the execution of the Do portion of the PDCA process. Senior leadership's lack of confidence in the feedback loops assigned to a process of *solution design* will only result in a stronger argument for increased structure, a return to *problem resolution*. Now you have a complete picture as to why a successful change process must be led (not promoted) from both the top-down *and* the front-lines-up.

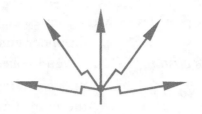

Our Capacity for Understanding

The final topic for us to address is one that I have mentioned a few times during our journey through Book Three, the *capacity for understanding*. Understanding forms, in varying degrees, the foundation for all forms of leadership (Books One and Two). Without understanding, there is no Purposeful form of change, only Glacial and Resulting. Understanding is what enables the co-existence, the balance (Leadership Rule #3) between the cultures of DO and WHY. It creates the ability for us to work smarter, not harder (Rule #2) and it is not possible for us to respect others, nor ourselves (Rule #1) if we don't make the time to first understand. So, what creates the capacity for us to understand? Answer: Our capacity for understanding is a function of our three lifelong companions; Change, Time, and Perspective. See Illustration #10 below.

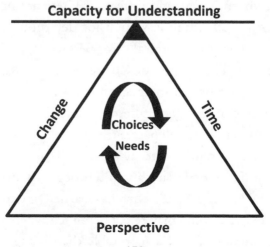

This illustration provides us with a representation of the process for understanding. Our individual and collective capacities for understanding are balanced on the point formed by the intersection of Change and Time, which are each supported by our Perspective. Notice which two catalysts are circulating within the support structure for understanding: human choices and human needs. Human

The Perspective(s) we choose to hold regarding Change and Time form our ability to tolerate anything which is new and/or different.

choice and need serve as the catalysts for how we perceive Change and Time. Do we view Change and Time as allies, enemies, or companions? The Perspective(s) we choose to hold regarding Change and Time form our ability to *tolerate* anything which is new and/or different. Here is an example of what I mean by this statement.

Jennifer and I have been recently blessed with a new granddaughter. As our newest member of the family entered the world, her capacity for understanding is pre-set at 100 percent. Everything, literally everything, to a newborn is new and different. There are no accumulated experiences forming a filtration system for determining what is, and isn't, acceptable. Every new arrival's Perspective regarding Change is one of acceptance. The process of Change is a necessary, welcomed, and constant companion. In the beginning, a newborn's capacity for understanding is completely unfiltered; therefore, their *tolerance* for change is at its maximum, 100 percent.

As a newborn becomes more aware of his or her surroundings, experiences begin to accumulate, and filters begin to form. Now, there are choices to be made. The newborn has learned to expect formula to be at room temperature and may reject being fed when its temperature is too cool. Being asleep is less acceptable than being awake, so they start fighting sleep in order to stay awake longer. When being carried, accumulated experience has now provided an expectation for the carrier to be standing and in a state of constant motion. Being held while the holder is seated and motionless is less acceptable, unless it is time for sleep, which has also been deemed to be unacceptable. Every new parent quickly learns that the newborn is no longer 100 percent tolerant of change and they are anxious to accomplish whatever is needed in order to produce Acceptable Results over Time. How is this parental learning process possible? A newborn only has one communication tool, their ability to cry. We'll get to this answer in a minute. First, we need to layer on the element of Time and how it interacts within our newborn example.

In the beginning, the concept of Time to a newborn is a function of need, not Perspective, and the needs are all pretty straightforward. It is either time to eat, sleep, be held, or have a diaper changed. Each of these four Time events are announced with an equal sense of urgency. The timeframe for addressing each need is *needs-based*, not *Perspective-based*. Because the newborn's perception of time is needs-based, when the need arises, the call for action is always NOW. When it comes to the concept of Time, a newborn has a tolerance level of 0 percent because they have a 0 percent capacity for understanding the source of the need. In the beginning, there is no process of choice involving Time. However, as experiences accumulate, the capacity for understanding expands and the tolerance levels for Time increase. Now the little one is gaining Perspective regarding Time and may choose to spend just a few more minutes enjoying the motion of the swing before reporting that it is time to eat.

As the newborn gains more control over their environment, they begin to learn Perspective, which is formed by their accumulated experiences. The newborn's capacity for understanding which types of Change are acceptable, and which are not, is narrowing. Their decreased tolerance for Change tracks their choice to narrow their capacity for understanding, and as a Result, they become less tolerant of the new and/

or different. As experiences accumulate, the same direct relationship is occurring related to the new arrival's tolerance of Time. It is just moving in the opposite direction. A growing capacity for understanding the concept of Time is resulting in a higher level of tolerance. Notice the interaction of the catalysts of Choice and Need within this simple example. As the role played by Need fades, the role of Choice grows. The newborn is acquiring Perspective related to both Change and Time.

The actions of a newborn are wonderful reminders that people are people, no matter where you find them. We all share the same basic, hard-coded choices and needs. We all access the Cycle of Human Development for growth. We are all products of our accumulated experiences and the influences of the cultures with whom we connect. What separates us, one from another, is our capacity for understanding, our ability to tolerate Change and Time based on Perspective. Allow me to make another point using our newborn example. For help in making this important point, we will turn our attention from the newborn to the new parents. Every new parent quickly learns to do whatever is needed in order to produce Acceptable Results over Time. Earlier we asked the question: "How is this parental learning process possible?"

The newborn has only one communication tool, their ability to cry. Yet, that one ability creates within the parents a new vocabulary of change. The parents are taught, by experience (accessing the Cycle of Human Development) that a certain pitch, volume, or sound contained within a baby's cry indicates which need or choice is to be addressed. One type of cry communicates: "I'm hungry. Fix it," whereas a slightly different cry indicates: "I am uncomfortable. Fix it." There is a cry for pain, a cry for sleep, a cry for stand up and keep moving, etc. and etc. Each new type of cry increases the parent's capacity for understanding, and with it, their tolerance of the cry. Brand new parents jump into action with every noise and cry. New parents, with more experience, develop tolerances and say things like: "She's alright. She's just being fussy." But, you let the pitch change to the "I'm hurting" cry, then get out of the way because Mom and Dad are on the run. Interesting, isn't it? So simple, but yet so illustrative. There are dozens of excellent examples of human behavior to be explored when you sit down and really think about the interactions between new parents and a newborn. Before I move on, I want to make one more point regarding the relationship between a parent's capacity for understanding and their tolerance for the new and/or different.

Think about a restaurant or any type of contained setting where you are mixed in with the public. You are seated at your table and a baby begins to cry. If you have the Perspective gained through parenting, how many times have you casually commented after hearing the cry: "Someone is upset?" Or said: "Sounds like someone is tired." However, if that cry changes to an "I'm in pain" message, observe how all the other parents turn toward the little one to see if they need help. Tolerance for a baby's cry is rooted within the accumulated experiences of parenting, which shapes Perspective, creating additional capacity for understanding. This higher level of tolerance will usually not be found within those who have not been exposed to the vocabulary of change taught by a newborn.

This newborn/new parent example is typical of human development. Think back to the Cycle of Human Development from Books One and Two. Once the parent's accumulated experiences, gained through Results over Time, have transformed Information (illustrated in this story by the baby's cry) into Knowledge, the resulting Skills become part of who they are. Notice that in our restaurant example, the Skills acquired through accumulated experiences remained

Knowledge, which has been acquired, but not tested through experience becomes an intellectual reference point, not a Skill. Intellectual reference points fade over Time, whereas acquired Skills, formed through accumulated experiences, remain with us.

with those who have been parents. The inexperienced diners hearing the baby's cry will not be making comments like: "I remember reading about this type of cry..." Knowledge, which has been acquired, but not tested through experience becomes an intellectual reference point, not a Skill. Intellectual reference points fade over Time, whereas acquired Skills, formed through accumulated experiences, remain with us and are always top of mind.

As time passes for the new parents, more experiences accumulate and Understanding grows. Ultimately, Understanding progresses to the point where they will accept a Modified Purpose due to their newly acquired Perspective. And, what is another way of describing the ability to accept Modified Purpose? Answer: The ability to accept a Modified Purpose can only occur when an individual has increased their tolerance for Change. Notice how we are beginning to see that all of these concepts and models are interconnected and build on each other? Let's continue.

As the little ones grow, and their awareness improves, they will acquire Perspectives and tolerances through parental example and their own accumulated experiences. Recall the "Hot! Don't touch!" lessons from Book Two. Their new Perspectives help them to develop more of a balance between their tolerances for Change and Time. Their capacity for understanding Change begins to slowly narrow while their choice to tolerate Time expands. Deep within the trenches of parenting, this is when everybody starts to settle into a routine. Parental sleep becomes possible. Both parents and newborn settle into a new level of "normal" which will last as long as it takes for the little one to discover the next learning opportunity.

Here is where this all gets really interesting. Take the new parent/newborn example from above and revisit the Capacity for Understanding model which is repeated below.

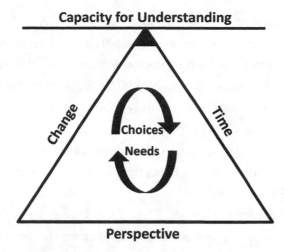

Takes on a whole new meaning, doesn't it? Now, take your new understanding and revisit the concepts put forward by the Results over Time model repeated below.

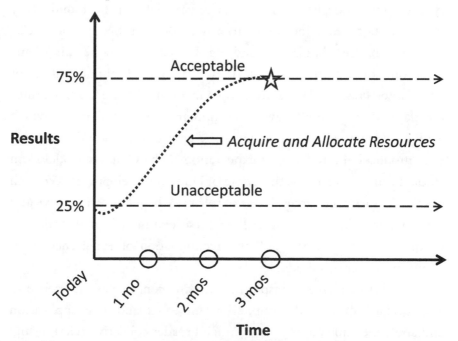

Think of the resources being allocated by the parents and consumed by the newborn in order to accomplish the demanded tasks via *problem resolution*. In the beginning, immediately following the birth of the baby, there is no time for *solution design*. PDCA with a newborn? Impossible. However, *solution design* has played a significant role in the stockpiling of resources in preparation for the new arrival, which represents the application of Purposeful Change. During the initial stages in the process of change immediately following the baby's arrival, the amplitude and frequency of the waves will increase rapidly, consuming resources at an alarming rate. As Perspectives change and the Capacity for Understanding (for all parties) increases, an environment of improved tolerance develops. At this point enters the opportunities for planning and for *solution design*. This is the settling in period and now begins the new parent's opportunity to plan for the next step and the step after that.

The newborn/new parent example is only one of many which could be used to illustrate how these concepts all work together. This same type of interaction between the various models can be found every time you start a new job, move to a new location, begin a new relationship, change schools, etc. and etc. Heavens, the same thing happens, only on a much smaller scale, when your cell phone shatters or your laptop crashes. People are people from the day we are born until the day we die. We all have basic human choices and needs which evolve over Time. They are shaped by environmental and economic circumstances and reflect our expectations (The Culture Model from Book Two). We all access the Cycle of Human Development. We each possess, in varying degrees, levels of tolerance based on Perspective and Capacity for Understanding. All of these common human traits are uniquely constructed through the accumulation of experiences over Time to form the individual.

Now that you have a grasp on these basic concepts as they relate to an individual or a small group, allow me to expand their application and apply the same concepts to a much broader collective relationship. We are ready to not only explain cultural differences, but to anticipate cultural developments. Here is where we combine our learning from all three books into a single application of Understanding.

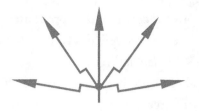

First Understand and Then Teach

The Transformational Leadership Model (Book Two) is built on a foundation of Understanding. In fact, the foundation for each leadership type is formed by Understanding. At the top of the Transformational Leadership Model, we find Results. Results are balanced between outcomes focused on Quality or Finance. We now know that forming the foundation for our capacity for understanding are the Perspectives we develop through experiences. Our capacity for understanding, our tolerance for Change and Time, is supported by the Perspectives we acquire as we accumulate experiences. Just like we discovered in our new parent/newborn example, as growth occurs along the Cycle of Human Development, the needs-based perception of Change and Time is replaced with a Perspective-based perception. The Results over Time graph enables us to visualize the consumption of resources as Unacceptable Results progress toward Acceptable Results. The ability to achieve Acceptable Results serves to increase our capacity for understanding. Increasing tolerance levels allow the process of PDCA to evolve from one of pure *problem resolution*, driven by Resulting Change, to one which combines *problem resolution **and** solution design*.

Solution design is driven by Purposeful Change which allows us the freedom to inject innovation, new purpose, into the Results over Time process. Innovation leads to the more effective use of available resources, or improved environmental and/or economic circumstances, leading to expectations for continued improvement. The three cultural elements have now been improved as a result of choices made based in Purposeful Change's *solution design*.

Now enters the all too predictable impact on culture development resulting from a protracted period of time filled with continued success, rapid change, *and/or* accelerated innovation. Think back to the Perspectives shared by the RB, SBB, and RMS executive leadership teams. These are all examples of human tolerances being modified after only a few short years of continued success. What happens if an entire birth generation is born into and raised within a protracted period filled with continued success, rapid change, *and* accelerated innovation? What cultural norms should we expect to see develop? How? Why? Answer: Let's go back to those responsible for shaping the building blocks for all cultural development. We are talking about those gathered at the kitchen table, the family unit.

Given the cultural circumstances framed by our question, the new parents of each subsequent birth generation, beginning with the Millennials, have access to unprecedented levels of resources. In fact, the parents of the Millennials had the ability to allocate enough resources to effectively modify the traditional Perspective-based *choices* made by their children regarding Time. The necessity for newborns to learn *choice* was suppressed because this new generation's parents were determined to use their resources to create what I will term as a *wants-based* perspective of Time within their children. The developing child was not given the opportunity to develop the Perspective required to learn *choice* through accumulated experiences. As a Result, many members of the new generation spent their formative years never knowing the difference between the hard-coded *needs-based* (fix it now) and the *wants-based* (deliver it now) perspective of Time. Next, add to the mix of recently taught wants-based intolerance the impact from readily available and rapidly advancing technology. This technology provides an endless set of convenient, inexpensive, and easily used devices and applications designed for and marketed toward the POS (the individual) in order to create enhanced value to the customer. Is this beginning to sound familiar to you?

The key to understanding the impact these changes will have on the Results over Time model for current and future generations lies in the evolving definition of two words: "value" and "customer." Value has historically been recognized as being created when the perceived benefit from a good, service, or experience exceeds its perceived cost. Value was, and still is for many, perceived as *production-based*. Value is *produced* when an acceptable result is delivered over an acceptable period of time, and is accessible within the constraints of available resources. This definition of value is reflected within the discussion of Results Ideology found in Book Two.

> *Value has historically been recognized as being created when the perceived benefit from a good, service, or experience exceeds its perceived cost: production-based.*

Through the application of technology and the subsequent production of new forms of resources, the accepted definition of value has been expanded within the two most recent birth generations. For these two groups, value has evolved beyond its historical, production-based limits of being a real/tangible good, service, or experience. Within the last two generations, value has been modified to include the perceived benefit exceeding the

> *Within the last two generations, value has been modified to include the perceived benefit exceeding the cost of either a real or virtual good, service, or experience.*

cost of either a real *or virtual* good, service, or experience. This is the new definition of "value." But what effect does it have on the end user, the "customer"?

In Book One, we discussed the impact on both Direct and Indirect Relationships generated by the creation of the new *virtual* relationship sub-category. The introduction of *virtual* value carries with it the same type of impacts on the culture (the collective customer) as it has on relationships. Virtual, by its very nature, encourages unilateral choice. There is no longer a need to communicate a shared purpose nor a need to attempt to gain a consensus through a shared understanding of purpose among the group. Every aspect of virtual value is geared toward reinforcing the individual's want-based perspective of Time. Because it doesn't require human collaboration of any type, the want-based perspective delivered by virtual value does not create the shared, accumulated experiences needed to increase an individual's capacity for understanding. Actually, the consumption of resources created by virtual value has just the opposite effect. The more virtual experiences consumed by an individual, the lower their tolerance level for any Change process or Time allocation, which is not of their own design. And, given the direct relationship between tolerance and the capacity for understanding, or the more virtual experiences consumed by future generations, the lower their capacity for understanding will become.

> *Virtual, by its very nature, encourages unilateral choice. There is no longer a need to communicate a shared purpose.*

The less tolerant the individual customer becomes, the more motivated they will be to seek out the want-based comforts provided by anything virtual. It is basic human nature to take the path perceived to be the least difficult. Unless interrupted by a catastrophic cultural event, this spiral of lower and lower tolerances will continue. What I have just described has already given rise to the significant cultural influences produced by the ideology based on Intent (Book Two). Some examples of the influences produced by the dominant role played by Intent Ideology would be: the power over society granted to political correctness (sanctioned cultural intolerance); the consumption of unaffordable resources in order to meet the demands of a culture geared toward a wants-based value system (witness the uncontrolled growth in personal and, especially, government debt, which is at $22 trillion and climbing); and the total dominance within society of the Resulting Change process, using problem resolution, vs. the infrequent use of the Purposeful Change process coupled with solution design.

As technologies improve, virtual experiences become an increasing percentage of each individual's Acceptable Results over Time. Why? Two reasons. First, there is the growing percentage of the population which views Time using the wants-based perspective. And second is the decreasing cost of the resources needed to access anything virtual. Assuming access to a reliable internet service, virtual experiences can be delivered to your location immediately, in an almost unlimited supply. If you assume the typical fixed-rate monthly cost for internet access, the more virtual experiences you download, the greater the perceived value. The devices used to process virtual experiences are rapidly decreasing in cost, while exponentially increasing in quality and capacity. Device manufacturers such as Apple, Microsoft, and Samsung are providing us with innovative solutions and ever-increasing ways to access higher quality virtual experiences.

Facebook, Google, Twitter, etc. are all the latest marketing companies serving as the next iteration on an old business model. These are the marketing channels for virtual experiences linking the want-based customer to the experience providers. Conceptually, what these cutting edge tech companies are doing is nothing new. I believe their basic business model was best expressed in the 1800s by a quote associated with an American experience provider named P.T. Barnum. Mr.

Barnum is credited for saying: "There's a sucker born every minute." Meaning, there are always those ready to accept the promise of a fantastic benefit, in this case more and better virtual experiences, delivered for the "low-low price" of almost nothing. Mr. Barnum promoted circus and sideshow experiences while collecting nickels and dimes in advance. These modern-day equivalents to the carnival barkers from the 1800s are promoting virtual experiences while collecting your personal data and selling it. Monetizing your personal information is their method of collecting nickels and dimes on an enormous scale. The business models used by Mr. Barnum and by Facebook, for example, are constructed around the same basic concept, but due to the wonders of technology, the experiences being offered today are delivered on a scale Mr. Barnum could have never imagined.

Here's the problem. Today's customer is less prepared than customers from previous generations for the challenges presented by experiences constructed around, and delivered through, the use of a virtual platform. In the pre-1970 cultures, if the production-based value of the experience didn't measure up, you simply used it to add to your capacity for understanding through perspective-based choice. Example, if the food at the circus made you sick, the next time you may choose to not eat so much or to eat different things. If the smells coming from the elephant tent were unpleasant, choose to avoid the elephant tent the next time. When you paid two dollars to have the experience of seeing the incredible Ape Man from the deepest jungles, only to discover it was nothing more than an actor wearing a cheap gorilla suit, you learned production-based value from the experience. Each accumulated experience (taste, smell, and sight) became part of your perspective as a developing child, increasing your capacity for understanding. You learned the benefits of making better choices because you experienced the consequences of making poor ones.

As you and your friends shared these experiences, their information combined with your own, becoming a base of knowledge on which you could construct a better experience the next time the circus came to town. I know my example is completely outdated, and that is the point. No matter how far back you go in cultural development, the benefits of shared, real experiences (positive or negative) form the foundation of human growth. Okay, want another example? How about your experiences the last time: you bought a car; rented an apartment; went fishing; played golf; changed jobs; went to the grocery store; etc.? You get the idea. We learn and grow through the experiences gained by living life on the front lines.

The key takeaway is, an experience doesn't need to be fantastic or incredible to create benefit for the culture. It just needs to be real and shared. Where is the primary point-of-service for the sharing of real experiences? Answer: in the trenches, on the front lines of life, within the family unit. Much like our definitions of Trust have needed to evolve (Book One) to accommodate increasing populations and distances, the way we define the family unit has evolved. I would suggest that we need to think of family in terms of those in proximity to you, very similar to the way we think of Trust, beginning with yourself.

> *The key takeaway is, an experience doesn't need to be fantastic or incredible to create benefit for the culture. It just needs to be real and shared.*

You are at the center of the concentric circles that make up the visualization of our family units. At the very core of the family unit, represented by the solid small circle in the center, is yourself and those who reside in the trenches of life with you. These people, those in the center of life with you, are the first to benefit from each experience. The family core usually consists of yourself and a spouse, partner, siblings, children, parents, and/or guardians. Those who reside in the next circle, the first group beyond the core, are more distant family members, close friends, and trusted advisors. Still further out, residing on the next circle, are extended family units which are co-workers or members of the broader community where you live and work. On the outermost circle are those extended family members which have yet to be discovered. These individuals are unknown to you, today. Through new experiences, you may discover that these unknown family members share a common bond with you, such as national pride, service in the military, love of the same hobby, etc.

We learned in Book One that relationships can migrate between types (Indirect becomes Direct, Business evolves to Personal, etc.). Proximity to the family core can also migrate. For example, face an emergency and complete strangers who reside on the outermost circles (first responders, ER physicians, nurses, or clergy) are immediately transported into the innermost circle of family. This example is one where the migration inward is immediate and can be temporary. Far more common is the gradual migration of family status which is based on the growth of productive relationships. The more frequently real experiences are shared between individuals, the greater the resulting capacity for understanding, producing increased tolerances, leading to more shared experiences, drawing others closer to the family's core as familiarity and trust increase. With the sharing of real experiences, migration takes place, moving others closer to the family core, strengthening the family unit. The sharing of virtual experiences does not facilitate understanding, and therefore, does not produce migration toward the family's core.

Now, let's think about the impact on the Results over Time model when using real, shared experiences vs. the sharing of virtual experiences. In particular, note the polar opposite impact on our tolerance levels. Using the Cycle of Human Development, we know that basic human nature is designed around our ability to develop enough knowledge and

> *You don't share a virtual experience; you encourage others to subscribe to it.*

skill to continually modify purpose through choice. This development enables us to maintain the balance between Change and Time and support it with the modified Perspectives. The input provided by the family unit after a shared experience plays a critical role in shaping each individual's Perspective. Real experiences lend themselves to the sharing process where virtual experiences are designed and marketed to influence the individual. Virtual experiences are designed to circumvent the family unit, not strengthen it. Typically, you don't share a virtual experience, you encourage others to subscribe to it. This action fractures the existing family unit. It serves to generate additional subscribers who provide new data profiles, which generates additional revenue for the new generation carnival barkers who are imploring you to enter their virtual tents. It is my opinion that the virtual experience industry has been designed to erode the core of the family unit down to a single person, yourself. Once the customer is isolated from the traditional family support structure, they continually provide the individual with virtual input designed to satisfy the demands created by their wants-based perspective of Time and value. This is a brilliant business model. First, create an artificial need within the customer, then meet the newly established need with virtual value. Unfortunately, the Results over Time generated by the virtual experiences industry have a negative impact on the family unit, which flows through to impact the broader culture.

As a culture, the natural balances required to maintain our capacity for understanding are under direct assault, and in many cases, no longer exist. The historic role of the family unit has been under a direct assault and is showing all the signs of erosion. In today's culture, Change is generally perceived as an ally, a weapon to be wielded in order to defeat the object(s) of our intolerance. You wake up one morning and an historic statue that has stood in the park for over a hundred years suddenly offends you in some way. Solution, tear it down. After all, our wants-based intolerance has taught us that historic significance is no longer relevant, nor are the perspectives held by others. Change is necessary not because it creates value, but because it removes the object of our individual, wants-based intolerance.

When we are out of balance, Change is an ally and Time is perceived as an enemy to be defeated through the application of more technology and additional resources. Virtual experiences have taught the individual, now holding a wants-based perspective, that additional resources should be free for them to allocate toward whatever result they wish to accomplish. As a result, many pockets of today's society are no longer aware of, nor do they care about, the processes involved within Results over Time. They exist within the *fix it NOW, no matter the cost to others* mentality generated by their wants-based perception of Time. There are many visible results we can observe which have been created by the intolerances produced through an out-of-balance capacity for understanding. One significant result is the growing voice of the Intent Ideology and the increased restrictions implemented by a culture built on a foundation of DO.

If asked to label and illustrate Intent Ideology's wants-based perception of Time, I would offer Illustration #11 below. The illustration would be labeled Resets over Time.

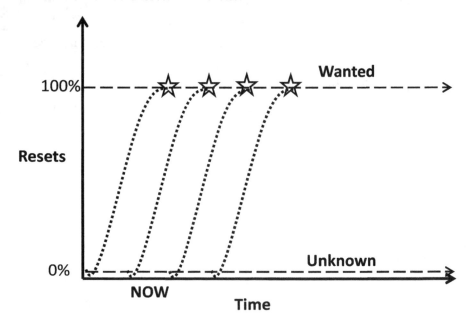

Notice there are no longer thresholds indicating Acceptable and Unacceptable Results. Those measurements have been replaced with Wanted and Unknown. This change represents the two very different Perspectives, Results vs. Resets. The Results model uses Acceptable and Unacceptable thresholds which reflected the *needs* of the CORE. The Resets model incorporates Wanted and Unknown thresholds which reflect the current *wants* of the individual.

> *The Results model uses Acceptable and Unacceptable thresholds which reflected the needs of the CORE. The Resets model incorporates Wanted and Unknown thresholds which reflect the current wants of the individual.*

In both models, the steep slope of the resource line indicates the consumption of resources in order to accomplish the established goal. However, where the resources consumed in the Results model are of a more traditional mix (labor, inventory, bricks and mortar, cash, time, etc.), the resource mix for the Resets model is heavily weighted to the consumption of only time, and within the Resets model, the expectations established for the consumption of time are pre-set using the references provided by virtual experiences. Those implementing the process of change through the use of the Resets model expect, actually they demand, the desired Wants to be accomplished immediately. These expectations, acquired through virtual experiences, establish the wants-based Perspective of Time, which promotes intolerance.

Notice the resource line abruptly ends at the point where the Wants are satisfied. This abrupt end illustrates the fundamental difference between the benefits offered by the use of a Results model vs. the benefits offered by the use of a Resets model. Even when an accomplished result is attained through the use of *problem resolution*, it still provides continuing benefit as the quality of the result deteriorates over time. In the case of an accomplished Want, using the Resets model as our guide, there are no residual benefits from the invested resources. An accomplished Want only generates a reset, at which time the accomplished Want is replaced with a new Want and the consumption of resources begins anew. This is the fundamental "Why" behind the accumulation of $22 trillion in national debt we discussed toward the end of Book Two. All of those borrowed resources, *plus* all of the taxes collected by the federal government during the last two birth generations have been consumed and we still have poverty, racial discrimination, a broken health care system, uncontrolled immigration, and drug addiction. Intent Ideology has grown to its current level of prominence within our culture simply because its purpose is to perpetuate existing wants by never actually accomplishing any form of solution.

At this point, I could go into another by-product from the wants-based perspective of Time and discuss the differing causes of stress between a culture which sees value in terms of Results over Time vs. a culture which views it through the prism of Resets over Time. But, my word count within Book Three is limited, so I will attempt to summarize the differing causes of stress in just a couple sentences. The stresses felt by individuals adhering to a Results model are based on the perceived need to accomplish multiple benefit-oriented tasks within the constraints of cost. Stresses felt by individuals adhering to a Resets model are based on the perceived need for them to identify a continuing supply of Wants without regard to benefit or cost. This is why we have created *safe spaces*, environments which suppress the introduction of different/new ideas on college campuses all across the US. The need for these spaces is just one example of the many protective actions taken by our current culture designed to shelter the unprepared young adults (the snowflakes) from the realities of experience gained through their interfacing with the front-lines life. The wants-based perspectives, the intolerances taught through the accumulation of virtual experiences, combined with lack of real, front-line experiences enabled by well-intentioned overly protective parents have combined to form a protective cocoon.

Please take special note of the following. I have had the opportunity to gain front-line experiences from leading many members of the Millennial generation. These experiences have been both personal and professional. Know what I learned? These are some of the most talented and dedicated individuals I have ever had the pleasure to lead. The key to unlocking their considerable potential centers on your actions aligning with your words. They need you to model for them the relationship elements of Trust, Integrity, and substantive Communication. And, in order for your words and actions to register with them in a meaningful way, all of your teaching needs to occur on the front-lines where they reside. I just wanted you to know that there are ways to successfully tap into their enormous potential.

Let's return to our discussion of wants-based stress. The objective of safe spaces and many other similar creations is to maintain the protective cocoon of childhood for as long as possible. There is a word which is commonly used as a description for all manner of well-intentioned protective actions designed to keep the population "safe." That word is *restriction*. Restriction has many culturally acceptable forms: regulation, legislation, policy, procedure, political correctness, etc. How about if we just called *restriction* enhanced *structure* around the process of change? DOes that ring any bells? Of course it DOes. You now know that we are dealing with Intent Ideology being used to satisfy a growing population of individuals possessing a wants-based perspective of time living within increasingly restrictive structures created by the culture of DO. And, what is needed to balance out the process of change when the culture of DO is in control? Answer: a new purpose offered by those willing to lead change from the top-down and the front-lines up. Over the last fifty years, the culture of DO and its ideology of Intent have capitalized on the weakened family unit.

The family unit has been eroded by several causes, but as I have demonstrated above, I believe the primary cause of the decline in the importance of family is the increasing influence of virtual experiences. The reduction of shared, real experiences has a direct relationship with our capacity for understanding. Decreasing amounts of shared, real experiences, resulting in a reduced capacity for understanding, reduces our level of tolerance for anything new or different, which begins the spiraling demand for more wants-based value delivered through virtual experiences. And, when you have a spiraling demand for value, there are always those who will be innovative and create new ways to satisfy the increased demand. All the modern-day carnival barkers need to DO is to draw you into their virtual tent with the promise of an endless supply of new, virtual experiences. Limitless benefits, offered for no apparent cost, creates a never-ending supply of Wants and Resets. All you need to DO to gain access to their tent is to conform to their restrictions, simply be willing to give up your freedom of choice to join the consensus, and accept the same Perspective as your fellow tent dwellers.

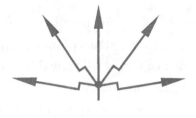

In Summary....

At the beginning of Book One, we began our journey with a transitional conversation where I stepped in front of a group of a couple hundred people I was about to lead. To start the process of creating productive relationships with those I was about to lead, I raised my hand and assumed responsibility for future Results over Time. As a member of the Results Ideology, my willingness to take responsibility, to hold myself accountable for results, was simply a part of who I was (and who I am). However, my willingness to assume responsibility for all future failures, while promising to pass along the credit for all future successes to others made me different. Different, not better or special, just different. What created the momentum for change, what granted me influence, was the alignment of my actions with my words.

At the beginning of Book Two, I stepped in front of a group of individuals whose lives had just been turned upside down by the announced sale of their banking locations. This was an opportunity for cultural transformation. I began the transformational conversation by raising my hand and assuming responsibility. Once again, my willingness to assume responsibility for all future failures, while promising to pass along the credit for all future successes to others, made me different. Different, not better or special.

During each of these two conversations, I began with thanking the audience for their time and attention followed by my promise not to waste either. By acknowledging the importance of their time and attention (attention being their freedom to choose to listen or not to listen), I was offering them my respect. Showing respect was my way of recognizing the value of their real, front-line experiences.

Book Three also began with me raising my hand, but in this conversation, I did not yet have the capacity for understanding intolerances. I was raising my hand in an effort to offer knowledge gained through front-line experience in order to help those at the top of the RB organizational chart. If you boil my action down to its very core, I was seeking respect for my accumulated, real, front-line experiences. The fact that there was a single member of the culture of WHY seated at the head of the table when I raised my hand was luck, or fate, depending on your Perspective.

While growing up on the farm, I was forced to learn how to change my perspective in order to survive, placing into motion a series of choices which led to accumulated experiences. These experiences helped me to develop, over time, my own capacity for understanding. Once you have learned to enhance your own capacity for understanding, never stop learning! The best way I have found to accelerate the learning process is to teach. You will never learn a subject more intently than when you are preparing to teach it to others. The role you assume as a teacher is irrelevant. Parent, spouse, friend, caregiver, guardian, coach, volunteer, professor, classroom instructor, or corporate leader: all of these examples, and many more, are where you will find the greatest opportunities to increase your capacity for understanding through teaching. And when you teach, maximize your benefit from the experience by teaching as close to the front-lines of life as possible. It is there, teaching in the trenches, on the front-lines of life, where you will discover the greatest diversity of perspectives, the most purposeful change, and the true value of time.

"First Understand and Then Teach." These are the first five words written at the very beginning of *LIVE better LEAD differently* (Book One). When I wrote those words about three years and two hundred thousand published words ago, my hope was to create a series of three books that would redefine our perspectives regarding relationships, culture, and change. My goal was, and still is, to change the way we think about leadership, family, and the human experience.

Admittedly, my approach to writing these books has been different from the accepted norms. I wanted to share a few of my life experiences as a way to demonstrate "How" these human conditions function, and most importantly, to illustrate "Why" they work the way they do. Over forty-five years ago, I taught myself to view things differently. I learned how to change my perspective regarding my personal experiences on the front-line of life. That doesn't mean I see myself as better or special, quite the opposite. I know I am just different. If the ability to discover a different perspective, combined with three rules and a few simple models, can change the life of this farm boy from central West Virginia, I'll bet there is value in the knowledge for you as well.

In the opening for Book One, I wrote "First Understand and Then Teach" on to a blank sheet of printer paper. The visual created by my reference to the "blank piece of paper" was literal as well as symbolic. At that moment in time, I needed to organize my thoughts around a new purpose, one that would benefit my CORE of responsibility and begin the process of growth for those I was about to lead. The symbolic meaning for the reader was intended to represent the process of change based on new purpose. When change is required, set old perspectives aside and start with a blank page. Never forget your real experiences, but never allow your past experiences to restrict your ability to plan the future, nor should you allow them to narrow your ability to learn from the present. The

> *Never forget your real experiences, but never allow your past experiences to restrict your ability to plan the future, nor should you allow them to narrow your ability to learn from the present.*

new page is blank for a reason. The future is never written. When you mentally or emotionally pull out the blank page, and you are about to create a new purpose, make it a good one.

May I suggest that, at the top of that blank page, you write these words: "First Understand and Then Teach."

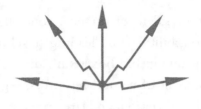

WHO IS ROB?

Based on my reading of many leadership books, it is customary for the author to provide information about themselves to the reader. This is as good a time as any to tell you a little bit about me. I have been truly blessed both with family and career.

I was born in Elyria, OH, in 1958 and lived in a couple different communities outside of Cleveland, OH, through the second grade. In 1967, Dad accepted a new job and our family of five moved to a small community in central West Virginia. In 1968, we relocated to a remote farm in central WV, which is where I grew up through high school graduation. I was the youngest of three children. Mom and Dad lived on that same farm, and loved it, until they passed away.

My wife of thirty-nine years deserves all the credit for what we have been able to accomplish together. We have one son. He is a civil engineer, who went on to earn his master's in management and has attained his PE certification. At the time I am writing this book, he and our daughter-in-law have been married for over six years and we have been blessed with one granddaughter. My wife holds a bachelor's degree in education. As for me, my formal education is a bachelor's degree in business administration with an accounting/finance major.

Over the course of my career, I have held various levels of responsibility, including but not limited to the following positions: chairman of the board of directors, chief executive officer, president, chief financial officer, chief administrative officer, chief innovation officer, executive vice president, vice president of finance, controller, etc. I have held these levels of responsibility while leading (teaching) within six different industries, including: big box retail, direct, commission-based sales, global development of natural resources, regional financial services, health care administration, and large project construction. These organizations spanned a range of ownership structures from privately held to publicly traded and from companies that were very much for profit to organizations with the tax designation of not-for-profit. I have attained multiple certifications in disciplines which include: leadership, sales, total quality management, re-engineering, and most recently, a lean practitioner.

As a leader within these differing organizations, my strategic objectives have varied, but I can summarize them for you by providing this brief list: turn struggling companies around while achieving financial and cultural stability; manage all aspects of accretive, sustainable growth, including growth by mergers and acquisitions; and/or leading cultural transformation resulting in enhanced, sustainable franchise value. In short, I have spent the majority of my leadership career as the person held accountable for positive results, and I am okay with that.

I have been a student of leadership and an observer of human nature my entire career. I enjoy the challenges of building an organization, and I love the process of helping others to grow. Believe me when I tell you that I am nothing special. I am a product of hard work and hard knocks. If I can succeed by applying the concepts presented in this book, you can succeed by applying the same concepts. To summarize, my purpose is pretty straightforward. I am here to help, and I am grateful for every opportunity to do so.

That's pretty much it. It is my deepest hope that you have found value in these pages and that I have been able to help you in some small way.

My thanks to you for providing me with a continuing opportunity to teach.

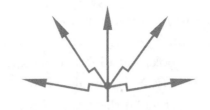

ACKNOWLEDGMENTS

I was the person at the keyboard putting these words onto the page, but with me stood a cast of hundreds who have helped me along the way. Allow me to begin by saying "Thank you" to the literary team, Larry Carpenter along with Clovercroft Publishing, without whom I would have never been able to take these words from the computer to the market.

My thanks to Jana and Jody at Maxwell Studios for the photography.

Website design and development, "LIVEbetterLEADdifferently-books.com," have been created by Bricks Without Straw. Thanks to Jamie and his team for all of their work.

My mom and dad have been gone for several years. They shaped much of what I am today, and for that I will always be grateful. A little over two years ago, Jennifer lost her mother. She was a second mother to me. I love her and I will always carry her with me.

During the drafting process for Book Three, the input and perspective gained from family was absolutely critical. Adam, Julie, Pam, and Dixie, to all of you I am very grateful for your guidance. Thank you!

There was one person outside of family who was key in helping me with the creative process, Sarah. Sarah is an accomplished executive and a very talented leader in her own right. From the earliest stages of all three books, Sarah encouraged me to share more of my personal experiences. She kept me focused on providing a more meaningful context for the reader. THANK YOU for your friendship, patience, and guidance!

Which brings me to the most important person of all, my wonderful wife of thirty-nine years, Jennifer. Without her support and encouragement, these books and a lifetime of experience would have not been possible. THANK YOU for everything I am and for all that we will experience together in the future. I am the luckiest guy in the world!